1

The User's Guide to Not Using

An Expert Guide to Recovery from Addiction

by
Dr. Jeremy Dubin,
D.O., ABAM, ABIHM

The User's Guide to Not Using
An Expert Guide to Recovery from Addiction

a YOURECOVERY ™ Publication
Copyright © 2012, E-Recovery, LLC

First Printing 2012

ISBN – 10: 0615688586
ISBN – 13: 978-0615688589

All of the cases described in this book are composites. They have been deliberately scrambled in order to protect patients' rights of confidentiality and privacy. No individual in this book corresponds to any actual person, living or dead.

ATTENTION CORPORATIONS, UNIVERSITIES, COLLEGES, REHABILITATION CENTERS, HOSPITALS, MEDICAL CLINICS, AND PROFESSIONAL ORGANIZATIONS: Quantity discounts are available on bulk purchases of this book for educational or gift purposes, or as premiums for increasing magazine subscriptions or renewals. For more information, or to request that Dr. Dubin speak at your event, write to info@yourecovery.com.

Cover graphic designed by Brian Weiss

Check out YOURecovery.com for additional resources, including Dr. Dubin's newsletter, "YOURecovery™ Tool Box."

ACKNOWLEDGMENTS

Thank you to my wife, Julie, for the feedback, the encouragement, and the support to get this stuff out of my head and on paper. I love you and am so grateful for our life together.

Thanks to my kids, Ben and Lily, for being my continual inspiration to share from my heart.

Thanks to Brian Weiss for the refinement of the messaging of the three core elements and the continual ethos of KISS—"Keep it Simple Stupid." You know how integral you were to this book getting done, thank you.

Thanks to Laura Portalupi for the invaluable editing improvements and thorough organizational recommendations – could NOT have done this without you, Laura.

Thank you to all my Dads—my biological dad, Barry, my stepdad, Steve, and my father-in-law, Rob. You each have been an anchor and a lighthouse to me at different times and for different reasons throughout my life. Thank you for your unwavering support.

To my fellow staff at Healing Arts Family Medicine—our quiet, and sometimes not so quiet, daily service we provide has created little miracles every week, often saving lives when it doesn't seem so apparent. Please know we do work to be proud of—from offering kind words to getting a urine test, know you have helped give hope to countless patients and their families. It is an honor to work with all of you.

Thank you to Judith Reynolds, M.D., ABAM who introduced me to addiction medicine and helped me see the need for access, good treatment, and compassion as a cornerstone of any successful recovery strategy.

To Scott Shannon, M.D., ABIHM, you have been my mentor in practicing Integrative Addiction Medicine. From your teachings on mental health and addiction to your clinical style to your nature as a human being, I thank you. I'd be lying if I said I haven't caught myself in a room with a patient saying to myself, "What would Dr. Shannon do right now?" You are a continual inspiration to practice from the heart and it is an honor to be your student, colleague, and friend.

To Fred LaMotte, my high school religious studies teacher, who introduced me to Eastern philosophies and the power of service, and who continues to enlighten, sometimes on a daily basis, through his poetry. Know you have provided quiet stewardship to me. Thank you.

To all of my colleagues that I have worked with professionally, you know who you are; we've understood the team approach from the beginning, and I thank you for helping make these success stories come true.

Thank you to Tony Spagnoli for the great formatting job, for turning messy drawings into coherent messages, and for bearing with a first-time author.

Thank you to all my patients who continue to be my greatest teacher.

" All you need is love."

-The Beatles

Dedicated to My Mom, Lois

The User's Guide To Not Using

An Expert Guide to Recovery from Addiction
By Dr. Jeremy Dubin D.O., ABAM, ABIHM

Table of Contents

" Love the life you live. Live the life you love."

−Bob Marley

NOTE FROM THE AUTHOR

What you are about to read was an accident.

When I was growing up I wanted to be a football player, then a firefighter, then a marine biologist. While my career aspirations changed many times, not once did I say, "I want to be an integrative family physician and an addiction medicine specialist." But, as they say, life is what happens while we are busy making plans.

My first exposure to addiction occurred when I was a kid. Every time my mother entered the hospital for her chronic medical conditions, she ended up in a second hospital afterwards. The facility had miniature golf, pool tables, large expanses of green acreage, and everyone walked around in robes and slippers. For an 8-year-old boy, the experience was fascinating, surreal, and hard to understand. It wasn't until sometime after I perfected a mean putting game that I realized my mother was in a rehabilitation center trying to manage her abuse of prescription pain medications.

I guess you could say that I had a crash course in addiction medicine at a young age. The chief lesson I took away was that not much worked to help my mother. In fact, instead of improving, she continued to get worse.

My mother died at 56 years old. Only when I was older did I realize how much her addiction had contributed to her overall health, or rather, ill health. Like many people whose loved ones struggle with addiction, I was angry, frustrated, and confused. I blamed the medical establishment as well as my mother, feeling shame and embarrassment that she couldn't "just get over it."

Becoming a physician was a next step in the attempt to understand, and ideally help, people suffering with this condition. I chose to be an Osteopathic Physician because I believed in the philosophy. I wanted to learn techniques to help people, not just treat the diseases they were suffering with.

My perspective that modern medicine did not have all the answers was eventually challenged, but not in medical school. Medical school actually reaffirmed my mistrust in what modern medicine could offer people suffering with addiction. Some people found long lasting answers via conventional means, but the majority I saw did not.

So, in an effort to gain a more integrative education, I started the student chapter of the American Holistic Medical Association during my first years of medical school. We brought midwives into obstetrics lectures and learned about acupuncture during neurology lectures. Integrating alternative strategies into evidence- based medical protocols became an important facet of my medical training.

Tenets of Osteopathic Medicine

1. The body is a unit; the person is a unit of body, mind, and spirit.

2. The body is capable of self-regulation, self-healing, and health maintenance.

3. Structure and function are reciprocally interrelated.

4. Rational treatment is based upon an understanding of the basic principles of body unity, self-regulation, and the interrelationship of structure and function.

Copyright © 2003-2010 American Osteopathic Association

Upon graduation from medical school, I was equipped with state-of-the-art tools to help people that were broken or bleeding. I knew how to deliver babies, perform surgery, and administer thousands of medicines. I had been rigorously prepared to treat ailing patients with conventional medicine, and I had familiarized myself with the holistic alternatives. I was eager to begin helping people as a physician.

I chose a residency in Colorado Springs centered on quality family medicine. While the standard of care was impressive, we had to deliver that care hurriedly. In 15 minutes, we had to review lab reports, x-rays, and specialist recommendations; confirm preventive benchmarks; and provide tools for management of medicines, diet, exercise, tobacco cessation, and stress reduction. There was little time to take a holistic or integrated approach.

As I strove to offer my patients as comprehensive care as possible, I noticed that the one disease we were ill-prepared for was, not surprisingly, addiction. To make matters worse, 10-15 percent of my patient population was suffering with it, just like diabetes, hypertension, and high cholesterol. What medical tools could I use to care for these patients? I had a few medicines, and I could refer people to Alcoholics Anonymous (AA), Narcotics Anonymous (NA), or a psychiatrist. When appropriate, I referred them to an inpatient rehabilitation unit or detoxification facility. I wish I could tell you that THAT was the end of the story—that these patients received treatment and entered recovery, never to turn back.

In reality, I saw them six to 12 months later, after their treatment had ended. More often than not they were still gripped by their addiction. They were suffering with a condition that, statistically, was shortening their lifespan by 20 years,[1] daily increasing their chance of overdose, and exacerbating their already existing chronic diseases. The issue was not that the treatments were inherently ineffective, but rather that the "cure" rate for addiction was somewhere around 15-25%.[2]

We would never accept those numbers with diabetes or hypertension. So why were we so complacent when it came to addiction?

Our philosophical and cultural history seemed to cause most of us to devalue this population and view addiction as a moral problem, not a physical one.[3] I will always remember the

1. McLellan, A.T., et.al., Drug Dependence, a Chronic Medical Illness Journal of the American Medical Association. 284: 1689-1695, 2000.
2. Graham, Allan W., et.al., Principles of Addiction Medicine, 3rd Edition: 2-15, 2003.
3. JAMA, 2000.

moment that highlighted this misguided perspective for me. While I was doing an emergency room rotation in residency, we were unable to resuscitate a 28-year-old female student who had overdosed on Oxycontin™, a long acting opiate. The attending physician's first comment was, "Can you believe it? She went to college and everything." Aside from the understood sad loss of a life, there seemed to be a sense of disbelief in the room, as if people were wondering, "How could this happen to someone like us?"

After realizing that I lacked the tools to fully support my patients suffering with addiction, I decided to pursue certification by yet another board. During residency, I became board certified in Addiction Medicine by the American Society of Addiction Medicine (ASAM).

Following more than a decade of training and experience, three board certifications, and personal experience with a loved one suffering with addiction, what had I observed?

In 2003, the Journal of the American Medical Association (JAMA) confirmed that "Addiction is poorly understood by clinicians." As a result, less than 1 percent of all medical school curricula addressed diagnosis and treatment of addiction, physicians failed to adequately screen for addiction, and medical professionals believed interventions were mostly ineffective (JAMA, 2003,290, 1299). Ironically, only three years earlier, JAMA defined drug dependence and drug abuse as a chronic, relapsing disease, just like diabetes or chronic obstructive pulmonary disease/COPD (JAMA, 2000).

I had observed that what works for one person does not necessarily work for another. In fact, a plan that proves useless to one person may be another's best tool for sustained recovery.

Applying this knowledge, I founded one of the first integrated outpatient treatment centers in the West. We offered real strategies through both alternative and conventional approaches, allowing people to safely create their own recovery stories.

As patients pursued treatment plans that worked for them, regardless of how orthodox or unorthodox, they began to get better. Real long-term recovery strategies began to emerge, strategies that could be successful interventions for a lifetime. People that had been unable to create effective sobriety began to see recovery that lasted weeks, months, years, and finally, decades.

As a family physician, I was seeing a variety of people who had already embarked on their road to recovery. Their success stories were unique. They had completed rehab 20 years ago, perhaps benefited from prescription medication, started attending NA or AA, found that perfect mixture of herbal or botanical supplements, or gotten out of an unhealthy relationship. These were people who had made significant headway by finding what worked well for them, but just as important, what didn't work.

When it came to helping my patients achieve more stability in recovery, I was not always telling them anything new. Many times, I was simply reminding them what strategies and health modalities had worked for them in the past and coaching them on how to integrate those elements into their lives now and in the future.

" Yesterday is gone. Tomorrow has not yet come. We have only today. Let us begin."

–Mother Teresa

INTRODUCTION

" It seems hopeless...I have never felt so frustrated in my life. Nothing seems to work."

Lisa I., 49 years old, leaving her son's rehabilitation clinic for the third time in four years

" I am desperate. No matter what we do, she won't, she can't stop drinking."

Richard R., 43-year-old husband of Liz, who suffers with recurrent alcoholism

" He takes the pills for pain, but I know he is taking more than he should, and I think he's been lying about it. He gets so angry when I bring it up...I feel so frustrated."

Mary W., 37-year-old wife of Chris, mom to Jason and Matt

" Rehab after rehab, he just can't stop doing drugs. I feel like it is hopeless; we are out of money to help him. I don't know where to turn next."

Sally T., 57 years old, speaking about her 22-year-old son Jack

Today's population suffering with addiction is not the demographic of the 1960s and 1970s. What was once confined almost exclusively to a destitute and poorly educated population now exists in mainstream America: the 36-year-old working single mom, the 57-year-old lawyer, the 21-year-old college student.

Addiction is a truly complex disease.

It demands an integrated approach with conventional medical tools, evidence-based addiction medicine principles, and an open mind to holistic and complementary strategies.

This book is based on the belief that long-term recovery is possible for every individual and that your recovery plan is whatever combination of treatments works for you.

Most people need a level of professional evaluation and an opportunity for detoxification in a secure residential setting to prepare the long-term tools necessary for a sustained recovery from addiction. This book is not intended as an alternative to professional evaluation or residential treatment. Rather, it is meant as a guide and resource for creating your long-term recovery plan. It is meant to remind you that your recovery exists and may include multiple approaches, some of which may not have taken full form yet.

I have seen countless success stories, each unique. Let yours be one of them.

What This Book Says—"The Bottom Line"

If you read nothing else in this book, read the remainder of this introduction. Recovery is not easy, but it is also not hopeless. There exists a light at the end of the tunnel, even though that tunnel may often seem narrow, rocky, and long.

Unit 1

Chapter 1 will help you figure out if you are truly addicted to something or if society is just telling you that you are. This may sound counterintuitive, but defining why people, and specifically you, use or abuse drugs or alcohol, is an important first step to real recovery. You may not even have a problem.

That's right. You may get past Chapter 1 and then give this book to someone who really needs it. I am not condoning drug or alcohol use but simply pointing out that a distinction exists between functional and dysfunctional, healthy and unhealthy...addicted and not addicted.

Chapter 2 is designed to help you deepen your understanding of yourself and how to start forming your lifelong recovery plan. This chapter also introduces the three essential components that serve as the foundation for long-term recovery.

Unit 2

Unit 2 elaborates on the three essential components to true long-lasting recovery. The components reflect the strides we have made in addiction research as a scientific community, as well as the commonalities I have observed between conventional and holistic addiction medicine strategies.

Chapter 3 may be the most important chapter in this book. Freedom from addiction demands discipline and commitment to your sense of purpose. Being ready to change and knowing why you want to change are necessary components to reaching real recovery. Your motivation has to start from within, not from an angry spouse or fed-up parent. It must be personal for it to be real. In other words, why are you here what are you here to do? Often, this is not a grand goal, like becoming President or climbing to the summit of Everest. Most goals are more personal than that. Being a good parent, spouse, son, or daughter; playing more music; finishing school—these are just a few examples.

Chapter 4 is about the fundamental human need for connection with others. Most people need support from another human being. One who can provide feedback, encouragement, and coaching to achieve long-term recovery. Understanding which people in your life are ready and willing to support you and which people are holding you back is key to a long lasting recovery strategy.

Chapters 5 and 6 discuss addiction as a chronic disease that, if tackled as such, can lead to full recovery. Research into brain changes after years of drug or alcohol abuse shows that there is a definite biochemical component of addiction; this component must be addressed to set the stage for real recovery. Addressing these brain changes can take shape in many ways, from medicines and nutraceuticals to exercise and nutrition.

Chapter 7 tackles the subject of relapse. In order to thrive in recovery, it is imperative that you accept that addiction is a chronic and potentially relapsing disease, not just an impulse control problem or bad behavior. (This does not mean you are excused from legal consequences or accountability for your actions.) Recovery success rates go up only when addiction is treated as a chronic disease and people are not deluded into thinking that it was an acute event or that it will pass quickly like a minor ankle sprain.

Chapter 7 also addresses the role of co-occurring disorders, from chronic pain to mental health issues including depression, anxiety, post traumatic stress disorder (PTSD), mood disorders, and attention deficit disorder (ADD). Many people suffering with addiction experience one or more co-occurring disorders. If these disorders are not addressed in a comprehensive way, long-term recovery will remain difficult to maintain.

Unit 3

Unit 3 is comprised of Chapter 8, which provides an integrative tool kit of potential strategies and health modalities for recovery. Use this chapter to identify strategies that you may want to integrate into your personal plan for recovery. While this is not an exhaustive list, it does provide insight on the most common strategies, both conventional and alternative, that have the most evidence to date.

Unit 4

Chapters 9 and 10 are designed to help you ask the right questions of yourself and equip you with tools to hold yourself accountable on a daily basis. Often, you need to challenge your personal and cultural beliefs when it comes to creating real recovery. Healing modalities are diverse and have roots in a variety of traditions. Conventional medicine is often one piece of the puzzle, but it may not be the only piece. The habit of continual self-audit, in a safe and honest fashion, helps you figure out what is working and what is not. How you "stay on track" is imperative to long lasting recovery.

Addiction treatment works; it needs to be tailored to the individual, not just the disease. So, if it is time to change; time to find those last pieces of the puzzle; time to get better, be better, and stay better—if it is time to finally create your recovery story, YOUR OWN RECOVERY—then keep reading.

"Don't let other people tell you what you want"

—Pat Riley

UNIT 1

IS THIS BOOK FOR YOU?

It may seem counterintuitive to ask yourself, "Do I really have a problem?" But it's important to take an honest look at yourself and your unique situation if you haven't done so already. Are you captive in your life? Do drugs and alcohol revolve around you or do you revolve around them? It's not always outright addiction, but sometimes it is and sometimes it may be somewhere in between. Does that distinction matter?

Perhaps you are questioning the way you use prescribed medicines or the way you may "recreationally" use drugs or alcohol. You may be wondering, "Do I need help? A counselor? A doctor? A group meeting? A psychiatrist? An addiction medicine specialist? A pain physician? Rehab?" These are legitimate questions and they are not always easy to answer. However, answers do exist. In this unit, we'll take a look at some key terms related to addiction. Understanding what these terms mean and how they are or are not applicable to you will help you move forward in creating a recovery strategy—if that is what you need.

Keep in mind that cultural, religious, or philosophical beliefs affect our perception of what constitutes a "problem." But what it comes down to is what is dysfunctional versus functional.

In other words, what is problem use? What is abuse? Is there use without abuse?

There are conflicting theories on what constitutes the definition of drug use versus actual abuse. Definitions vary[1]:

Types of Use:

– Zero use (abstinence)
– Misuse
– Abuse
– Irregular use
– Prescribed use
– Illicit use
– Overuse
– Proper use

But, again, what is problem use?

1. Stewart, Sherry H., et al. Current Drug Abuse Reviews. 2008, 1, 255-262.

" This above all: to thine own self be true."

–William Shakespeare

CHAPTER 1

USE VS. PROBLEM USE

Let's start at the beginning. There are hundreds of substance abuse screening tools out there, and they all have their merits as well as their shortcomings. The Drug Abuse Screening Test (DAST) has been used in my practice for years and has always been a valuable tool in helping to identify substance abuse issues. The same can be said for the Alcohol Use Disorders Identification Test (AUDIT). This is not meant to single these tests out as the absolute best, just the best I've found in practice.

Go ahead and take these tests now if you are concerned about your drug and/or alcohol use. The results will help you ensure this book is for you. (See Appendix B)

<u>Key Terms</u>

Every drug behaves differently when it interacts with the human body. Each varies when it comes to tolerance; dependence, addiction, and withdrawal potential; and medical versus nonmedical risk. Understanding the following terms will help you understand where you are on the dependence-addiction continuum and how to move forward methodically, in a more efficient and deliberate way.

Tolerance
The body's ability to adapt to the continual presence of a substance, producing a gradual need to increase the dose to obtain the same effect.[1]

Often people become tolerant to the effects of a drug and need more of it or a different route of administration to get the same effect. This is a physiologic response and can happen to anyone, from Grandma to a drug abuser that lives on the street, or even a grandma who happens to deal drugs on the street.

Physical Dependence
Adaptation of the body to the long-term presence of a drug.[2]

Over time, the human body can grow accustomed to the presence of a drug. When this happens, the body needs to have that drug to avoid usual unpleasant withdrawal symptoms. This can be as subtle as a headache from not having your morning coffee to overt flu-like symptoms from heroin or opiate withdrawal. Any way you define it, when a drug that has been used or abused for long periods of time is discontinued suddenly, withdrawal symptoms occur. Withdrawal can usually be avoided by decreasing the dosage slowly before stopping altogether. Dependence does not always equal addiction. This will be discussed later, but it is important to begin making this distinction now.

Addiction
Compulsive use of a substance for psychic effects or in order to satisfy a craving.[3]

Addiction is characterized by the continued use of a drug despite harm to the user, such as legal or health problems, damage to relationships, or job loss. The compulsive need to get high from the substance can lead to rapid escalation of the dose. This differs from physical dependence, when there is a need for slower, periodic increases due to tolerance. Addiction is considered a chronic, neurobiological disease. Genetic,

---

1. Diagnostic and Statistical Manual of Mental Disorders, Fourth Edition, 2000.
2. DSM-IV, 2000.
3. DSM-IV, 2000.

psychosocial, and environmental factors influence the development and manifestations of addiction.

Pseudo-addiction
Drug-seeking behavior such as hoarding meds, obtaining drugs from more than one provider, frequent emergency room visits, or requests for dose increases because of unrelieved pain.[4]

This definition is an important one to understand. Often people think they are addicted to a substance because they exhibit addictive behavior (running out early of medicine, getting medicine from multiple health care providers, using the medicines differently than prescribed, etc.) Once adequate pain medication is prescribed and pain is controlled, the patient is able to comply with a prescribed medical regimen and the drug-seeking behavior stops. The diagnosis of pseudo-addiction can be a slippery slope. People must be careful not to deceive themselves. The line between addiction and pseudo-addiction is not always black and white; the same is true of dependence and addiction.

Often, these definitions take personal shape over time and are difficult to unravel in one office visit. But they are important to differentiate so that you can create the proper trajectory for the type of treatment you may need.

More detailed criteria can be found in Appendix C.

The Dependence-Addiction Continuum

The personal, as well as professional, evaluation of where you stand on the continuum between dependence and addiction—and pseudo-addiction—demands careful attention. The distinction is not always obvious, but a committed health care practitioner can help you navigate these terms.

As a family doctor who sees people anywhere from zero to 50 years after rehab, I've observed that dependence can move to addiction at any time, and at times, vice versa. Whether it's the medical use of marijuana, medicines at bedtime for

---

4. DSM IV, 2000.

insomnia and anxiety, or two beers at the end of the day, all dependencies have the potential to become addictions. A family history of substance abuse, a personal history of substance abuse, and/or a co-occurring mental health diagnosis greatly increases the likelihood of dependence becoming an addiction.[5]

Dependence ←——————→ Addiction

" Addiction doesn't come heralded by a band; it sneaks up on you, and sometimes with extraordinary speed"

-C. Everett Koop, Retired U.S. Surgeon General

Let me introduce you to Mary, an 83-year-old patient of mine. Mary took one Vicodin™ tablet every morning for her arthritis and a half tablet more when her grandchildren came over in the evening. She followed this routine for 22 years.

She never increased her dose, even when a mild increase would be expected due to physiological tolerance. When Mary's husband died, she came in to tell me that she had run out of her pain medicine early...for the first time. Upon further investigation, it became clear that her overwhelming grief and increasing anxiety due to a dire financial situation led her to use

5. McLellan, A.T., et.al., Drug Dependence, a Chronic Medical Illness Journal of the American Medical Association. 284: 1689-1695, 2000.

her Vicodin in a different way. Mary was now using her medicine to treat a coexisting mental condition, unbeknownst to her. To Mary, she was simply in more pain. So while the Vicodin™ was treating her anxiety, which was perceived as pain, she was becoming addicted.

I explained to Mary that when controlling anxiety with opiates, there is typically a progressively greater tolerance, leading to increased use and eventual abuse. Once a person is abusing the medicine, it becomes necessary to obtain it in larger doses and more frequently. For Mary, it was the simple description of these definitions that motivated her to return to her former daily regimen. Together, we explored other, more efficacious routes for treating her grief and anxiety.

Putting Drugs in a Cultural Context

Even with definitions and criteria, it is difficult to maintain objectivity about addiction. The consequences of addiction can be ugly and wide reaching. But, are drugs and alcohol inherently bad for you?

Drugs and alcohol have a significant presence in cultures worldwide, especially in spiritual and religious practices. Wine in the Judeo-Christian culture, Peyote in Native American cultures, the Coca leaf in various cultures in Peru and Ecuador, and Ayahuasca Root in Brazil are just a few examples. In short, people have used drugs and alcohol for thousands of years in all the same ways that they are used today: ceremoniously, recreationally, medically, and potentially dangerously.

The culture in which you grew up probably shaped your perspective on drugs and alcohol. By and large, culture determines the way that most of the people around you, i.e. society, perceive use and abuse of these substances. Understanding that culture is the way that a particular group of people organize the world, and therefore a relative concept, is a crucial first step in removing your cultural bias.

Your preexisting beliefs about drugs and alcohol, if not acknowledged and challenged, will hinder your full recovery. Why? You need to be honest with yourself and open to all strategies that may aid you in your recovery. If you have already formed an opinion about what you should or shouldn't be doing, you are severely limiting your options and chance at long-term recovery. In some ways, the "blackboard needs to be wiped clean," before you can better evaluate if there is a problem or not.

It is up to you to seriously reflect on the toll a substance is having on you. Here's a relatively extreme example that underscores the importance of understanding your own unique situation. For a lot of people, drinking coffee is a form of dependence. But for someone with a cardiac condition, the caffeine in that daily cup of coffee could cause a dangerous increase in heart rate. At the same time, there is a famous beatnik poet out there who was said to have used heroin on a regular basis until he died at 83 years old.

Problem use is defined by the individual, not by an arbitrary set of standards. Although this is an extreme example, you get the point. Heroin is ugly, right? It is illegal; can lead to higher rates of HIV and hepatitis; can lead to addiction very quickly; and is often associated with crime, destitution, desperation, overdose, and death. But when you put these associations aside, you can empirically look at the drug, whether it's caffeine or opiates (the addictive agent in heroin and most prescription painkillers), and you can see more clearly the difference between potential rates of dependence, tolerance, addiction, and medical risk. This is important because it allows you to evaluate yourself, not the disease you are told you have, or the drug you may be using or misusing. It becomes Mary with addiction, not "Addiction."

Ignoring a potential drug problem can be life-threatening for you and your family, not to mention tremendously costly to society as a whole. That's why it's important for you—not someone else—to determine whether you have a problem. The following graphs are not meant to condone any drug use nor try to portray some drugs as safer than others. Any substance can be dangerous to the individual and its impact on the human condition is not "one size fits all." These graphs are designed to reflect some of the differences observed in a broader sense pertaining to the aforementioned definitions in the context of specific drugs. They should be viewed as ranges instead of exact numbers, and need to be filtered through the complexity that is each person's use.

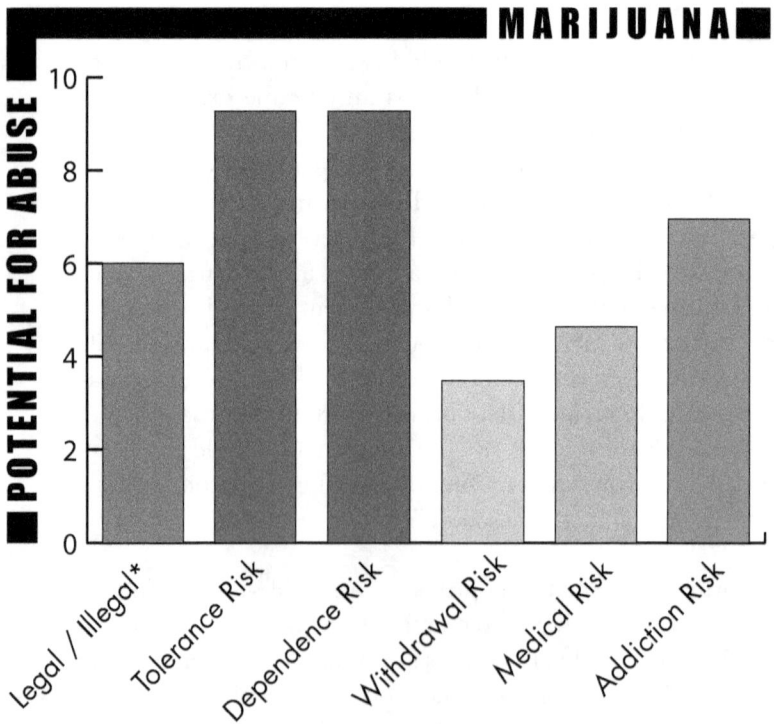

* Legal for recreational use in 20 states / still against federal law

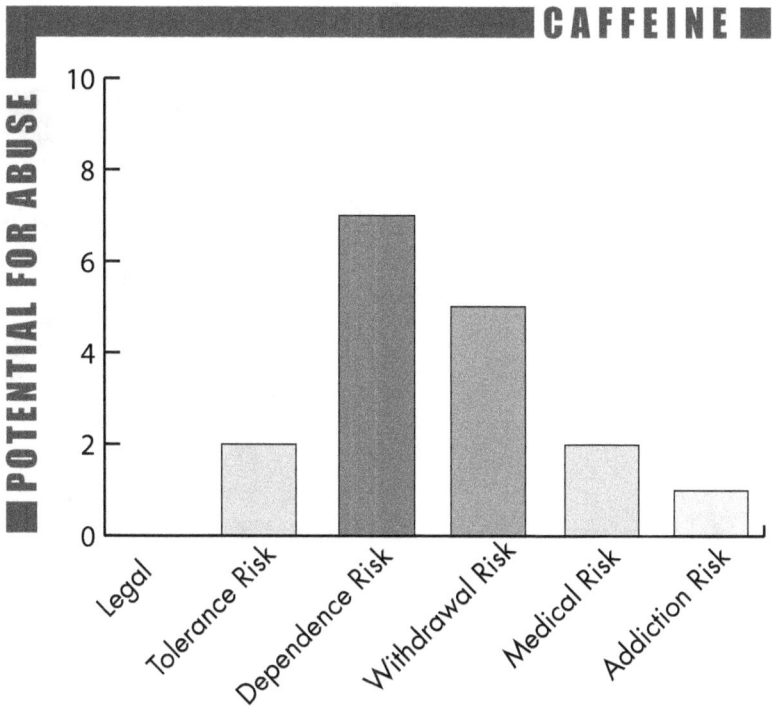

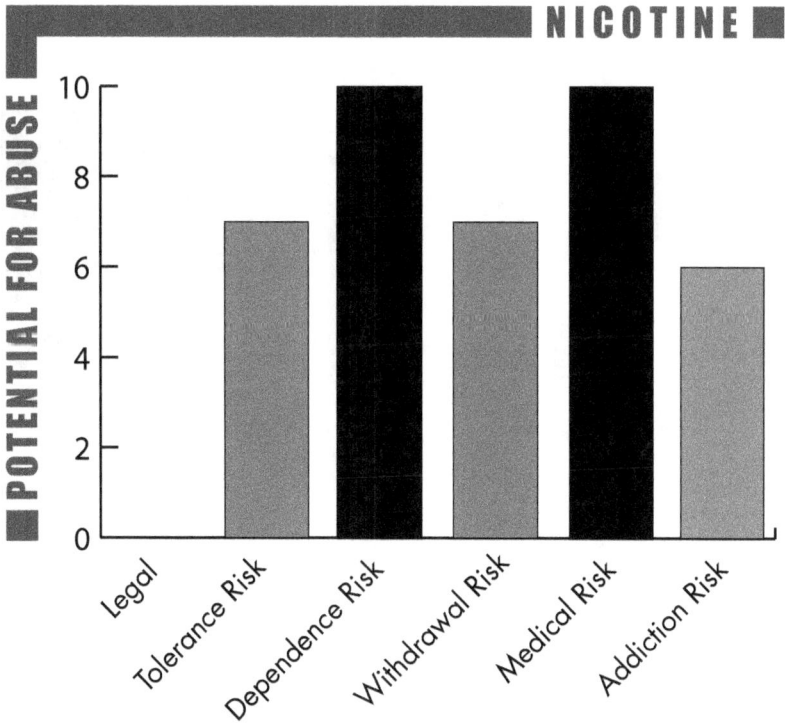

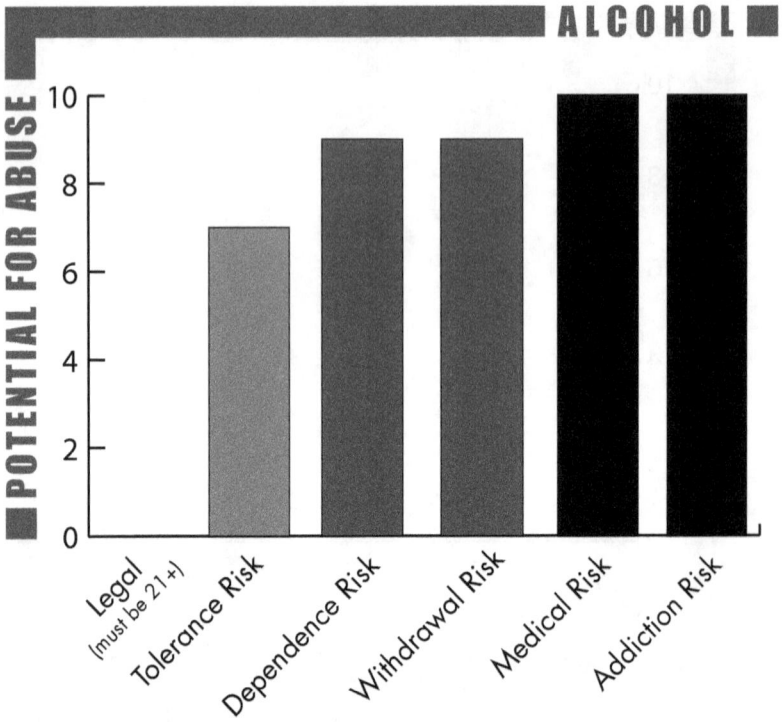

ALCOHOL

POTENTIAL FOR ABUSE

Legal (must be 21+), Tolerance Risk, Dependence Risk, Withdrawal Risk, Medical Risk, Addiction Risk

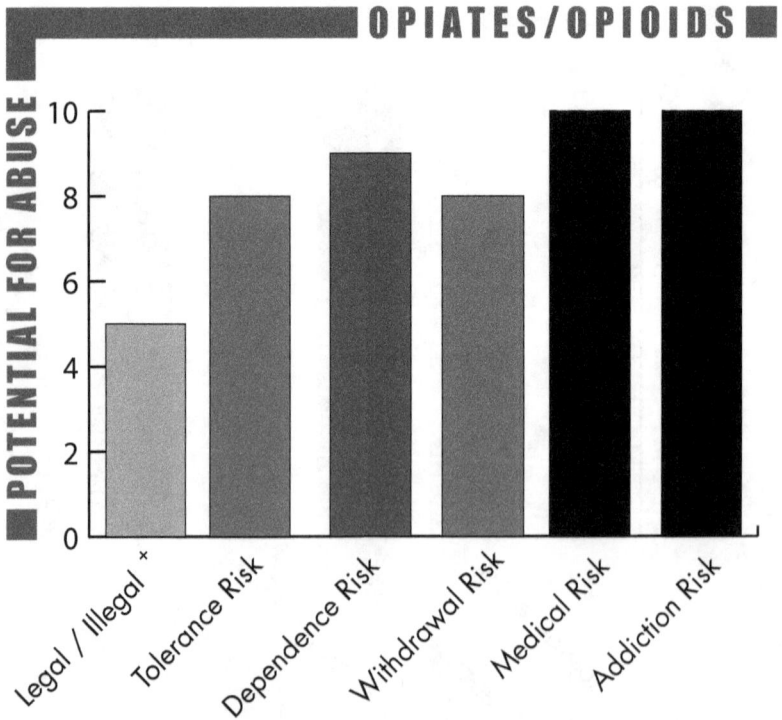

OPIATES/OPIOIDS

POTENTIAL FOR ABUSE

Legal / Illegal +, Tolerance Risk, Dependence Risk, Withdrawal Risk, Medical Risk, Addiction Risk

+ Legal by prescription for pain / illegal in form of heroin or abused Rx (Oxycodone, Hydrocodone, morphine, etc.)

COCAINE&METHAMPHETAMINES

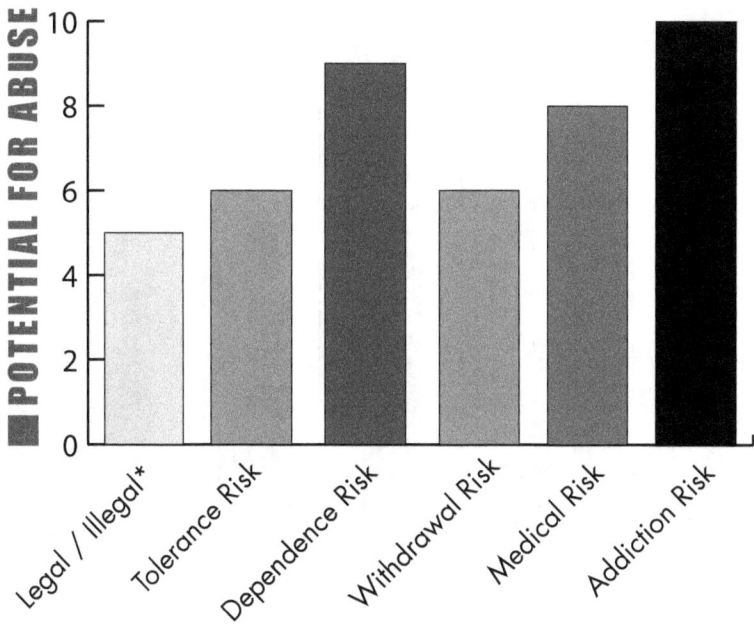

POTENTIAL FOR ABUSE

Legal / Illegal* — 5
Tolerance Risk — 6
Dependence Risk — 9
Withdrawal Risk — 6
Medical Risk — 8
Addiction Risk — 10

SEDATIVES & TRANQUILIZERS/BENZODIAZEPINES

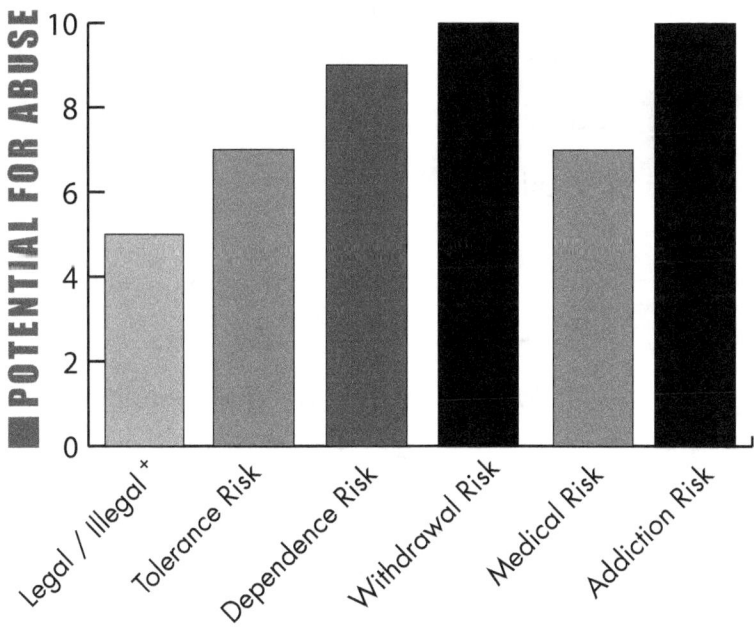

POTENTIAL FOR ABUSE

Legal / Illegal + — 5
Tolerance Risk — 7
Dependence Risk — 9
Withdrawal Risk — 10
Medical Risk — 7
Addiction Risk — 10

* Legal by prescription - Rx stimulants / illegal in form of cocaine, illicit meth amphetamine, and abused Rx stumulants
+ Legal by prescription - Rx benzodiazepines / illegal in form of abused Rx

31

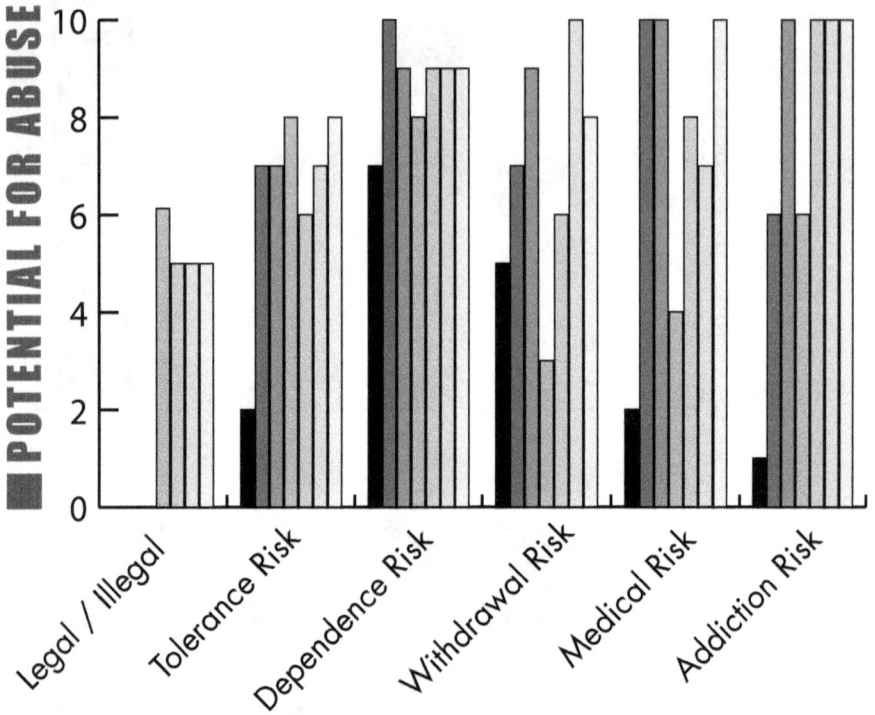

" If you change the way you look at things, the things you look at change."

—Dr. Wayne Dyer

CHAPTER 2

KEY COMPONENTS TO RECOVERY

If you have gotten this far in the book and believe that your dependency is problematic or that you are suffering with addiction, the next step is to increase your understanding. The more you understand yourself and human nature in general, especially what is out there that has really helped people, the easier it will be to develop a strategy for complete recovery.

First, let's take a look at some helpful information that's already out there.

You must be ready to make a change; if you are not ready, recovery is like pulling teeth. For every three steps forward, you will probably fall back two. Again, recovery is a very personal endeavor and must be tailored and fueled by the individual suffering with addiction. If a recovery strategy is created to placate another person (spouse, boss, child, etc.), it is almost always doomed to be short-lived and insincere.

The following is a useful model that helps describe the stages of change.

Stages of Change [1]

The stages of change are:

- Precontemplation (Not yet acknowledging that there is a problem behavior that needs to be changed)
- Contemplation (Acknowledging that there is a problem but not yet ready or sure of wanting to make a change)
- Preparation/Determination (Getting ready to change)
- Action/Willpower (Changing behavior)
- Maintenance (Maintaining the behavior change) and
- Relapse (Returning to older behaviors and abandoning the new changes)

PRECONTEMPLATION

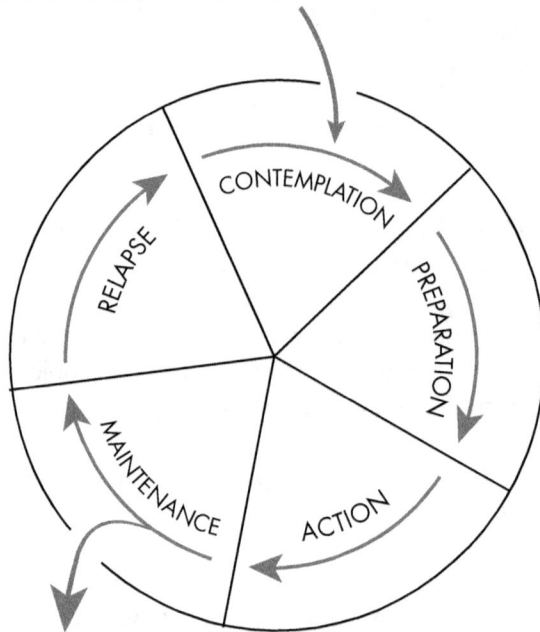

STABLE BEHAVIOR

The Stages of Change Model was developed in the late 1970s and early 1980s by James Prochaska and Carlo DiClemente at the University of Rhode Island. They were studying how smokers were able to quit. The model is an effective way to view change for those struggling with addiction of any kind.

---

1. Transtheoretical Model of Change, Stages of Change model. Prochaska and DiClemente, 1983

YOURecovery™ Wellness Wheel

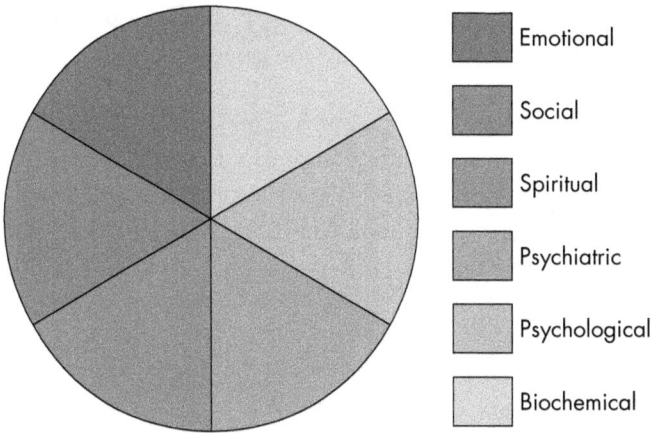

Legend:
- Emotional
- Social
- Spiritual
- Psychiatric
- Psychological
- Biochemical

Wellness as It Relates to Recovery

The goal in any long-term recovery strategy is to achieve a state of wellness. The term "wellness" has been articulated in diverse ways, from medical school textbooks to the underlying tenets of Chinese medicine. But what does wellness look like in the "recovery" field?

To synthesize all the wellness information out there, I've created a diagram that integrates my training and experience, especially as it pertains to people suffering with addiction.

No doubt you've heard wellness described in terms of mind, body, and spirit. But what does this actually mean in practice? It may be time to give some "meat" to these terms. In other words, people suffering with addiction need to take concrete steps to create their long-term strategy. Just saying, "you need a holistic approach" is not enough. What does that mean in reality? On a day-to-day basis?

The descriptions below will be covered in more detail later, but this is a good opportunity to start thinking about what a "holistic" approach really looks like.

Spirit can be defined as why you are here. This is often tied to your faith, religion, or spiritual beliefs—or lack thereof. I refer to the spirit component as "Purpose." Once you have started the process of defining your purpose, you are then ready to consider the body component.

Body can be defined as paying attention to the brain changes that have occurred after long-term abuse. Treatment of physiologic changes usually takes the form of medication, nutraceuticals, exercise, and/or nutrition. I refer to the body component as "Biointervention." Once you have begun to take care of your body, you can move on to the mind component.

Mind can be defined as your emotional stability. Individual counseling or therapy, group therapy, relationships with loved ones, and intimacy are all methods of caring for your mind. I refer to the mind component as "Interpersonal Intervention."

These three key components are prioritized differently in each person's recovery story and will be discussed in more detail soon; but for almost everyone, attending to each of these components is a necessary foundation for recovery. Keep in mind that the strategies presented in Unit 3, the YOURecovery™ Tool Kit, are not ancillary to these three components. In fact, modalities such as acupuncture, yoga, or hypnosis are often central to a final recovery plan. However, I have found that these core components of Purpose, Biointervention, and Interpersonal Intervention need to be solidly defined for the individual in order to experience real long-term recovery.

The graph below is a visual representation of the three core components: Purpose, Biointervention, and Interpersonal

Intervention.

YOURecovery's ™ 3 Core Components:

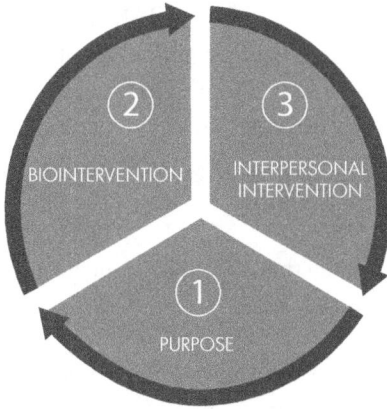

It is up to you to determine which component deserves high-est priority in your strategy. Typically, each component must receive a certain level of attention. This is different for every individual and can be defined as your "recovery threshold." Reaching this threshold is a great achievement, but ideally you will continue beyond the threshold and ultimately achieve "optimal recovery."

For simplicity's sake, a scale of 1-10 is used to compare the varying levels of importance each component plays in recov-ery. Remember, everyone who creates a recovery strategy has a unique "recovery priority scale."

Let's look at some examples.

Sarah, 28 years old

Sarah has a strong family history of depression and anxiety. Her parents were both hospitalized at early ages for mental health diagnoses. Sarah herself has been in and out of hospitals for most of her life. She found solutions with a combination of medications and nutritional supplements that stabilize her brain chemistry so that she can engage in other treatments.

Biointervention: 7 / 10

Sarah estimates that the biochemical component is 7 on her recovery priority scale.

Her experience with individual counseling yielded good results, and she has been able to scale back her counseling sessions to every one to two months. Concrete goals about relapse prevention strategies were worked out early and implemented specifically in the first year of individual counseling.

Most of her drug use was associated with her old roommates. She has since moved out, and she only sees them in rare social situations.

Interpersonal Intervention: 1 / 10

Sarah estimates that the interpersonal component is 1 on her recovery priority scale.

Sarah had her son Todd when she was 19. Her driving force is now being a good mother to Todd. It took her a long time to get custody after a bitter divorce and a history of legal problems related to her substance abuse. Sarah's main purpose in life is clear. She has found joy in making peanut butter sandwiches in the morning and attending play recitals. Sarah has worked hard for it, and this is her main reason to stay on track with her recovery.

Purpose: 8 / 10

Sarah estimates that the purpose component is 8 on her recovery priority scale.

SARAH'S RECOVERY

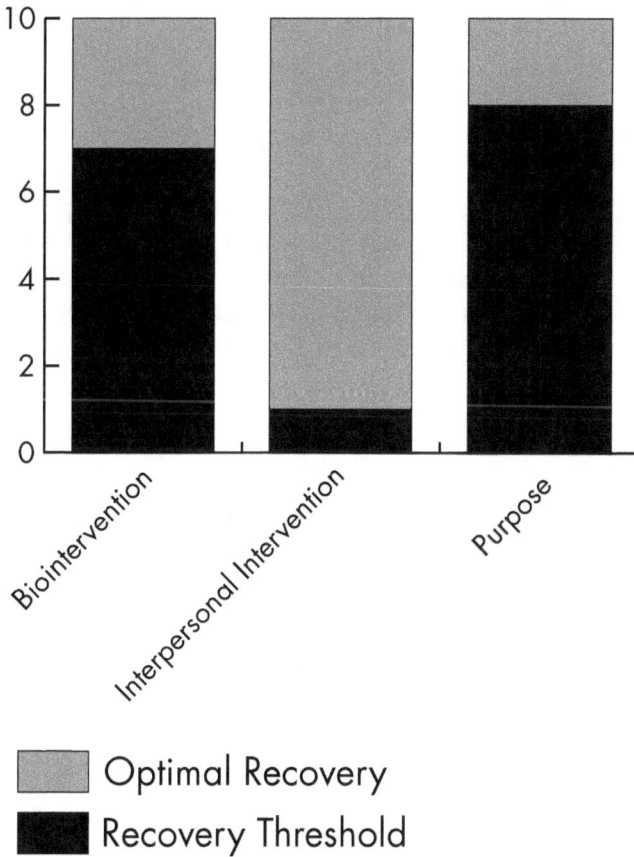

Bar chart showing values for Biointervention, Interpersonal Intervention, and Purpose on a scale from 0 to 10, with categories Optimal Recovery (gray) and Recovery Threshold (black).

- Optimal Recovery
- Recovery Threshold

Mike, 23 years old

After going through detoxification for addiction to metham-phetamines, Mike realized that he had gotten into the wrong scene at the wrong time. To combat his cravings, Mike followed a regimen that included a good amino acid complex, better nutrition, and daily exercise. His fatigue and other with-drawal symptoms subsided shortly after his stay in a detoxifi-cation unit. No other mental health diagnoses were unveiled, such as depression or anxiety.

Biointervention: 1-2 / 10

Mike estimates that the biochemical component is 1-2 on his recovery priority scale.

Mike's relationship with Carol began with the lure of drug use. It was not until he was able to remove himself from this partnership that real recovery began to take hold. Unfortu-nately, Carol has not made the choice to make changes in her life yet, and since they shared two dogs, there is moderate con-tact with one another.

It wasn't until Mike met Dr. B, a psychologist specializing in addiction and cognitive behavioral therapy, that he discovered the roots of his stimulant abuse. It was this interpersonal re-lationship that laid the firm foundation to engage in all other recovery modalities. Dr. B has been an invaluable partner in Mike's long-term recovery.

Interpersonal intervention: 8 / 10

Mike estimates that the interpersonal component is 8 on his recovery priority scale.

Mike always had "trouble" with being raised Catholic, but lately, going to mass with his mother on Sundays has really helped them reconnect. His mother has been a source of un-conditional love, understanding, and acceptance that Mike has really needed during a tough time in his life. When you ask him about church these days, he says, "It's growing on me. It helps knowing I am part of something bigger than myself."

Mike is also back in school for motorcycle maintenance, a degree he has wanted to finish for a very long time.

Purpose: 5 / 10

Mike estimates that the purpose component is 5 on his recovery priority scale.

MIKE'S RECOVERY

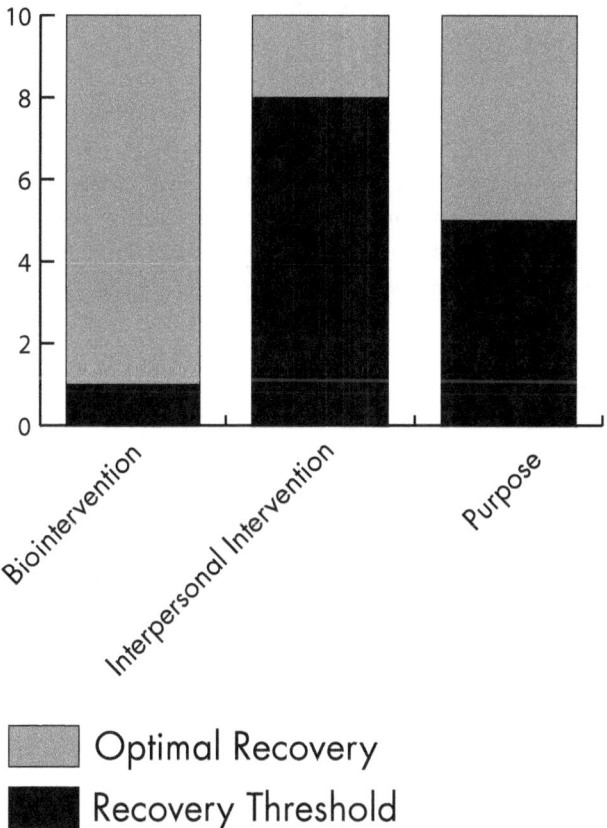

Optimal Recovery
Recovery Threshold

Lisa, 42 years old

It took Lisa almost 20 years to come to terms with her addictions, but she finally realized that depression and anxiety were the main reasons that drugs and alcohol were so alluring to her in the first place. When she takes her depression medication in the morning and her botanical supplement at night to help with anxiety, she finds herself more able to engage with her counselor. In addition to taking medication and a supplement, Lisa exercises for at least 20 minutes each day.

Biointervention: 4-5 / 10

Lisa estimates that the biochemical component is 4-5 on her recovery priority scale.

Lisa has been a self-described "loner" most of her life. She lives alone with her three dogs and is content with her living situation. There is not much social temptation in her life. She does not drug seek anymore and has lost all of her old contacts. Her main connection has long since moved away.

Lisa's counselor and AA sponsor have been very important allies in her recovery. Strategies they have created together have paved the way for long-term recovery. Lisa has found peace, solace, and solidarity in going to AA as much as she can. It grounds her and is an important daily reminder that helps her with transient cravings.

Interpersonal Intervention: 3-4 / 10

Lisa estimates that the interpersonal component is 3-4 on her recovery priority scale.

Lisa has long wanted to become a yoga instructor and finally found direction when it came to studying Eastern philosophies and practicing Buddhism on a daily basis. Although raised in a different religion, it was Buddhist principles and practices that have pushed her back into school. She is now driven everyday by what she wants to give back as well as by her daily spiritual practice.

Lisa estimates that the purpose component is 6 on her recovery priority scale.

LISA'S RECOVERY

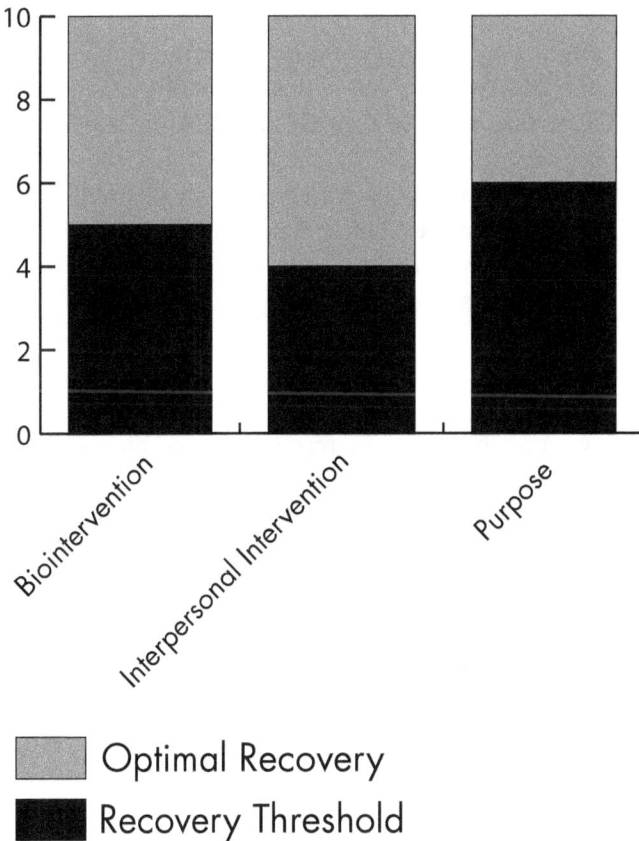

Jay, 27 years old

Jay has had trouble with alcohol and cocaine for most of his teens and 20s. It was not until he realized that he had been self-medicating for attention deficit disorder that he was able to challenge his addiction. Now that he is properly treating this condition with a prescription medication and behavioral interventions, his addiction has been kept in check.

Biointervention: 8 / 10

Jay estimates that the biochemical component is 8 on his recovery priority scale.

Jay is now in school in California while his old friends are back East. He does not have the same degree of temptation to use drugs or alcohol since most of his triggers were related to these relationships.

Jay got a lot of group counseling at the beginning of his recovery. It gave him solace to know that he was not alone in his battles and that other people just like him were having similar challenges. It was this understanding that allowed him to go from attending daily Cocaine Anonymous meetings to attending about once per month. For the most part, he is busy studying. He is surrounded by goal-oriented people who are busy with their academic research.

Interpersonal Intervention: 0-1 / 10

Jay estimates that the interpersonal component is 0-1 on his recovery priority scale.

Jay's main goal in life is to become a marine biologist, and he is currently in a Ph.D. program. He is very excited about his studies and looks forward to school every day. His professional development has overtaken his cravings for cocaine. When the cravings arise, he knows what to do.

Jay estimates that the purpose component is 8 on his recovery priority scale.

JAY'S RECOVERY

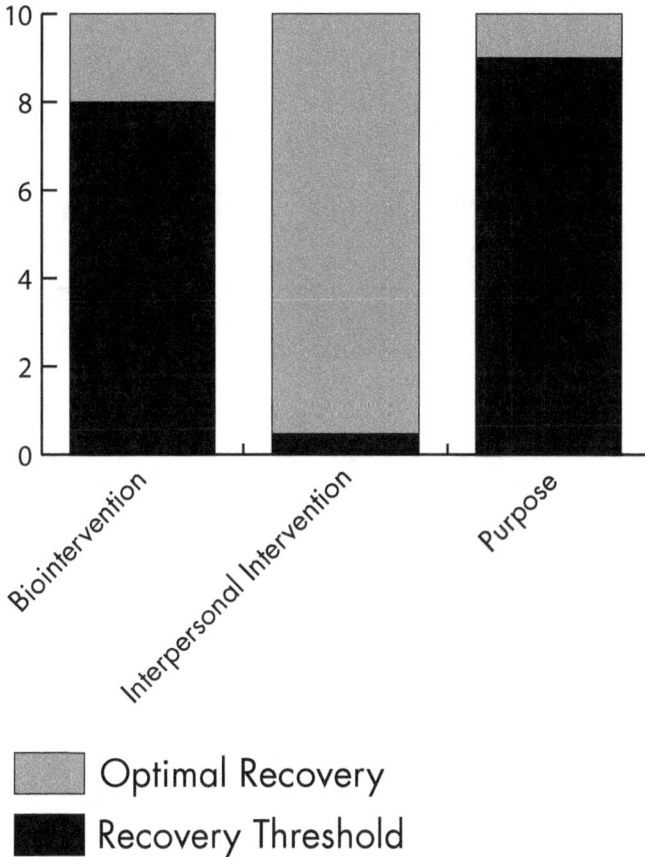

Optimal Recovery
Recovery Threshold

As you can see, recovery looks different for everyone. Priorities change, as well as the degree of importance these components play in different people's lives.

Here is a good exercise to get you started. Keep in mind that your numbers are allowed to change as much as you want, even on a daily basis—it is **YOUR RECOVERY!** What do you think your priorities are in terms of these three components? Be specific. Write down why you think one is more important than another. Give it some thought. Often, this is best done with someone that knows you (and ideally loves you), and is willing to give you feedback on what seems significant and what does not. You can come back to this as you read on as well, but I would challenge that you have some answers in there already. Compare the answers you give now with the ones you will give at the end of this book. This list is organic, it grows, it changes, and it becomes the strategy that is eventually your full and complete recovery.

Your Purpose Score: _____ / 10

(0 – Not that Important   10 – Very Important)

Why? Why do you want a life without drugs and/or alcohol?

_____

_____

_____

_____

_____

Your Biointervention Score: _____ / 10

(0 – Not that Important   10 – Very Important)

How much does your brain play a role? (Use factors such as nutritional status; amount of exercise you do; genetics or family history; time of abuse [greater than 6–9 months]; history of rehabilitation attempts; co-occurring depression, anxiety, or bipolar disorder; failed medication attempts, etc. to help you formulate this response.)

_____

_____

_____

_____

_____

Your Interpersonal Intervention Score: _____ / 10

(0 – Not that Important   10 – Very Important)

Who? How much do other people play or not play a role in your recovery? (Use factors such as living situation, peer involvement, support from loved ones, etc. to help you formulate this response.)

_____

_____

_____

_____

_____

Shades of Recovery

A trajectory leading to success looks different to almost everyone. The key is to be honest with yourself regarding what kind of outcome you want or inevitably need. In addition, you need to be honest with your family, your loved ones, and your health care provider to start filling in these blanks for yourself.

Knowing when to shift gears and utilize different or additional health strategies is a good sign in recovery. It means you are self-auditing well; you have moved beyond the shame or self loathing that is often seen in addiction. It means you have become recovery- and solution-focused, not addiction-focused. Recovery is about outcomes—not culture or preexisting belief structures.

Remember, the three core components of Purpose, Biointervention, and Interpersonal Intervention manifest differently in everyone. These ranks can change at any time and usually do change throughout a person's lifetime. Be flexible. Do not get stuck on what does not work, even if it used to work. Your recovery story reflects the ever-changing you. You and only you are entitled to be the author of that story. What's the first line of your success story look like?

_____

_____

_____

_____

_____

Be Bold. What does your successful recovery story look like in its entirety? Tell your story, even if it has not fully been told yet.

_____

_____

_____

_____

_____

_____

_____

_____

_____

_____

_____

_____

_____

_____

_____

_____

_____

" Every great dream begins with a dreamer. Always remember, you have within you the strength, the patience, and the passion to reach for the stars and to change the world."

—Harriet Tubman

UNIT 2

CREATING YOUR SUCCESSFUL RECOVERY

THREE CORE ELEMENTS

The three core components were introduced in the last unit, but let's take some time to break them down further. It's important that these terms are not empty phrases. They need to be meaningful to you. The good news is that most likely these answers are already inside you; the trick is to tease them out purposefully, fully, and honestly. Being authentic with yourself is not easy. The process will challenge your comfort level, but it will also lead to real answers, and ultimately—true recovery.

> *" Learn to get in touch with the silence within yourself and know that everything in this life has a purpose."*
>
> *—Elisabeth Kubler-Ross*

CHAPTER 3

WHY CHANGE? TAPPING INTO YOUR PURPOSE

Why do you want to stop using or abusing drugs or alcohol? Seriously—why not keep doing what you have been doing?

The answer cannot be "I'm just tired of this" or "I don't have the gas money to drive to Denver anymore." Your reason for entering recovery must be specific, well thought through, and articulated in concrete terms. The main purpose driving you forward needs to maintain its momentum today, tomorrow, next year, and ideally for the rest of your life. Here are some clearly articulated purposes identified by patients:

"I want my health back so I can be at my daughter's wedding."

"I want to be a better spouse."

"I want to be a better sibling."

"I want to be a better parent."

"I want to be a better child."

"I want to further my career or hobbies."

"I need a healthier strategy to treat my depression."

"I want to be in full control of my actions and decisions."

"I don't want to have another heart attack."

"I don't want to live in pain anymore."

Your purpose needs to be a personal reflection of why life would be better without substance abuse. This isn't about what someone else is telling you—it's only about what you identify as significant and meaningful to you. These self-identified purpose statements evolve, becoming more refined and specific. They can change to reflect bold revelations, or they can be as simple as something you want to accomplish today, something that further abuse would not let you do.

"I want to be there more for my son." ⟶ *"I want to make it to his school plays more consistently"* ⟶ *"I want to be there Tuesday afternoon for his presentation on Australia."*

Self-Love

When people ask themselves, "Am I a good father or mother, son or daughter, husband or wife?" it always seems to come down to another question: "Am I making a difference?" In other words, "What is my purpose?" This sense that "I belong here" or "I have something to do here" can lead to connection with others—a sense of selflessness—that can ease the transition into real self-love, and ultimately, self-care. Self-love must come from within. Although it feels good to get praise from external sources, you can't depend on that alone. It is difficult to make progress in recovery if you are continuously relying on another for your emotional stability. Keep in mind that most people face this challenge, whether they are in recovery or not. Getting to a place where you love yourself could take months or years. It is only through self-acceptance that you find self-forgiveness and real intimate relationships with others can begin to take root. Self-love is the first step to creating a strong safety net in your long-term recovery story.

The Importance of Self-Forgiveness

You must forgive yourself before you begin your recovery. This existential or psychological shift must occur before you can honestly assess yourself and create real goals that are fulfilling, provide self-support, and create success. Starting at this place is the foundation of 12-step programs. It is also the observation of people who have successfully created lasting long-term recovery. Think of it this way: the slate must be clean so you can start rewriting your book.

It can be challenging to move past the artificial shame that society has put on you for "becoming" addicted. It can be challenging to give up the "old" you, whose identity and perceived self-identification is intimately tied to your history of drug abuse. This does not remove accountability or consequence from your actions. There are social, interpersonal, and often societal consequences of dishonesty, criminal behavior, and a history of less-than-desirable decision-making; but, to start down the recovery path, you must let go of any shame you feel. If you continuously punish yourself for what you have done, you will not be able to explore the difficult choices, strategic revelations, and important goal setting necessary to your long-term recovery.

Starting now, define yourself with the action of today—not yesterday.

Why Purpose Is Important

There is a good reason to examine this core element first. Your purpose will give you strength and motivation during the hardest parts of your recovery. Unless your purpose is driving you forward, recovery is a very difficult road.

Your purpose can be anything. Your decision to choose recovery can be motivated by numerous factors. What may seem trivial to you may be another's most vital tool: because you want to be part of a working family; you want to be a more loving spouse, parent, or friend; you want to feel more in control of your life; you want to live longer; you are tired of being sick; you are in pain; you want to build birdhouses, be a botanist, work on that old car, paint, learn to fly planes. The list goes on and on.

Tapping into your purpose may be an essential key to unlocking the grip that addiction has had on you. When you are in touch with your purpose, addiction becomes a major obstacle to the fulfillment of that purpose. Without trivializing the potential deadly consequences of untreated addiction, it is very much like allergies. If some people do not use their saline nasal spray, take their antihistamine, and keep their bedroom windows closed at night, they feel miserable. They are ineffective at their jobs and too tired to participate as a spouse, parent, student, or member of society. In short, they are unable to fulfill their purpose. The same can be said about addiction. If you do not stick to your personalized treatment plan, relapse is close, and day after day is spent chasing elusive solutions instead of fulfilling your purpose.

Each person's purpose is different. Your purpose may lead you to a life of service, athletics, writing, parenting, being a good spouse, or caring for the environment. Whatever it is, your purpose must drive you. It must get you out of bed and excite you.

What are you fighting for? Take some time to reflect on this question. Then write out your purpose in a sentence or two.

Why Fight for Your Recovery?

_____

_____

_____

Return to this purpose as often as you need to. Keep in mind that recovery can begin in an instant, but if you haven't identified what you're fighting for, it is hard to find the fighter within.

Your Purpose in Context of the Greater World

Recovery often demands an attempt to embrace the concept that we are connected to something greater than ourselves—that we are part of something beyond our addiction. How you make sense of this is up to you. Whether you adhere to a religious doctrine in which you were raised, a newfound spirituality, or a belief in the interconnectedness of all people, it is important to remember that when you feel the most alone, you are not, and this is crucial to your long-term recovery.

" Life becomes harder for us when we live for others, but it also becomes richer and happier."

−Albert Schweitzer

CHAPTER 4

INTERPERSONAL INTERVENTION — THE IMPORTANCE OF RELATIONSHIP

People's histories are different, their lives are different, and their stories of recovery are different. Simply put, people recover in different ways. Still, most people need support throughout recovery. This support can take many forms, including the provision of feedback, coaching, or "safety nets" when needed. Your greatest supporter could be a friend, spouse, family member, group, counselor, doctor, or spiritual leader. The key is to find someone ready to go down this difficult road with you.

Support through Loved Ones

People need people. Often, it is a relationship that is about to be lost or a level of intimacy with another that is threatened before people take action against their addiction.

Consider this example of recovery achieved primarily through relationship with a loved one.

Janice had been using cocaine for over three years with increasing regularity to help her escape the misery of her marriage. Raising three children, she was married to a pilot who was rarely home. It was the reprioritization of intimacy with her husband via a regular Friday night date and marriage counseling that allowed her to create a successful recovery strategy. It took some time and a leap of faith to include her husband in her struggles, but after several months, Janice found she no longer had a cocaine problem. Counseling and date night were, and continue to be, her tools to battle cocaine cravings. In a way, you could say love saved her life.

Although this is a rare story of recovery in that interpersonal intervention was the only strategy utilized, it does exemplify the power of interconnectedness. The unconditional love and support provided by Janice's husband enabled her to create an authentic long-term recovery strategy. Do not underestimate the influence of loved ones in your recovery.

" He that won't be counseled can't be helped."

—Benjamin Franklin

Support through Therapy

The importance of individual counseling and/or therapy in the process of recovery cannot be understated. All but a few types of therapy supported by evidence show their efficacy in addiction and recovery. Along with exercise, good nutrition, group therapy, and attention to potential neurobiological changes, therapy with a certified addictions counselor or a licensed psychologist is typically vital to any successful recovery program. In this safe and honest forum, concrete strategies and goals, addiction survival skills, and recovery tools are created and audited for effectiveness.

Often, talk therapy is where you begin to build the real infra-structure for living in recovery. After you have figured out why you want recovery and after you have leveled the playing field biochemically, this is where the "hard work" starts. As much as you may want to believe you can do it on your own, people need each other. Counselors and Psychologists know what questions you should be asking yourself and how to guide you in answering them. There are many therapy options; several are described on the following pages.

Sometimes You Have to Just Push Delete

Part of your recovery will likely involve distancing yourself from certain people who will not be able to provide the support you need during recovery. Often, not socializing with these in-dividuals is initially challenging, but it may represent the be-ginning of a journey into self-care, or self-love. A loved one, licensed psychologist, addictions counselor, group meeting, or religious leader may be vital in helping you to understand who these people are so you can identify them as obstacles to your recovery and move forward accordingly.

Cognitive Behavioral Therapy (CBT)

Cognitive behavioral therapy is a form of psychosocial therapy that assumes that incorrect thinking patterns cause poor decision-making, self-destructive behavior, and "negative" emotions. The treatment focuses on changing an individual's thoughts or patterns in order to change his or her behavior and emotional state. It often plays a central role in the treatment of substance abuse disorders.

Motivational Enhancement Therapy (MET)

Motivational enhancement therapy challenges clients to find their own motivation for change. It then directs the client to create a personal, well-structured, and thorough plan for change. The approach is largely client centered, although planned and directed. In the context of addiction, MET seeks to alter the harmful use of drugs. Because each client sets his or her own goals, no absolute goal is demanded through MET, although counselors may advise specific goals such as complete abstinence. MET can provide clients with a template for small changes while a wider range of life goals may be explored as well. MET is based on principles of cognitive and social psychology. The counselor helps create a mirror for the individual, as to unveil the potential incongruity in the client's perceptions between current behavior and significant personal goals.

Schema-Focused Therapy

Developed by Dr. Jeffrey E. Young for use in treatment of personality disorders, Schema Therapy is intended for use when patients fail to respond or improve after having been through other therapies. It can also be used to treat major depressive disorders and other psychological issues of individuals and couples. Schema Therapy is a combination of many different therapy techniques, some of which include cognitive behavioral therapy, object relations, psychoanalysis, mindfulness, dialectical behavior therapy, interpersonal relation skills, discussion one-on-one, group discussion, and constructivism. Schema Therapy also borrows extensively from a range of theoretical concepts and methods from Transactional Analysis.

As opposed to some of the more widely known and popular therapy methods, Schema Therapy is most often used and considered a specialty form of therapy in the treatment of personality disorders, most commonly borderline personality disorder. Schema Therapy is based on a theory that childhood and adolescent traumas are the most likely causes of borderline personality disorder and other similar personality disorders. The approach of Schema Therapy emphasizes patients, psychiatrists, and therapists building bonds of trust with each other. This modality has been used successfully in the field of substance abuse.

Dialectical Behavioral Therapy (DBT)

A mode of treatment designed for people with borderline personality disorder (BPD), particularly those with suicidal behavior. Dialectical behavioral therapy aims to help people with BPD to validate their emotions and behaviors, examine those behaviors and emotions that have a negative impact on their lives, and make a conscious effort to bring about positive changes. In validation the therapist helps the patient see that his or her behavior and responses are understandable in relation to his or her current life situation. In BPD, however, these behaviors and responses often create a great deal of stress, suffering, and instability in the patient's life. With training in problem solving the patient works on building social and personal skills to deal effectively with the problems in life. Studies have indicated that people with BPD who have had DBT make fewer suicide attempts and enter the hospital less often. It is a modality often instituted with success in substance abuse treatment.

Group Psychotherapy (Integrated) – AA / NA

Group therapy is a form of psychosocial treatment where a small group of patients meet regularly to talk, interact, and discuss problems with each other and the group leader (therapist). From 12-step programs, such as AA or NA, to other types of non-AA group settings, group therapy attempts to give individuals a safe and comfortable place where they can work out problems and emotional issues. Patients gain insight into their own thoughts and behavior, and offer suggestions and support to others. In addition, patients who have a difficult time with interpersonal relationships can benefit from the social interactions that are a basic part of the group therapy experience. Groups are a cornerstone of most successful recovery plans.

Often, people are resistant to group interactions, especially at the beginning of treatment. This should be challenged. What I will say to patients that refuse to go to group therapy is that they don't have to talk if they don't want to. I urge them to see that 1) they need to do something different and they are coming to me for advice on what has worked for other people and what has not; 2) they can take "nuggets" of information—revelations, positive or negative—from hearing others people's stories, and it is up to them to figure out if they can be incorporated into their recovery strategy.

Family Psychotherapy

Family psychotherapy is a type of psychotherapy that validates the importance of the family unit in someone's overall recovery. It is designed to identify family patterns that may contribute to a behavior problem or mental illness and equips family members to deal with or challenge those habits. Family therapy involves discussion and problem-solving sessions with the family. Some of these sessions may be as a group, in couples, or one-on-one. In family therapy, the web of interpersonal relationships is examined and, ideally, communication is strengthened within the family. Herein lies the importance of creating intimacy with others when making one's strategy. Whether the roots of addiction can be found in family dynamics or strengthening current family bonds, family therapy is invaluable in that it can create a safe place for people in recovery.

61

Contingency Management

This is a type of treatment used in the mental health or substance abuse fields. Patients are rewarded (or, less often, punished) for their behavior. This is generally reflected by adherence to or failure to follow rules and regulations or their treatment plan. Incentives go a long way with all of us, especially with people who are at the beginning of their recovery journey. Knowing you may win an iPod if your urines remain clear from illicit substances for 30 days is enticing to some. Albeit somewhat manipulative, it can be supportive of a sober state where other interventions can take root that otherwise would be threatened by continued abuse.

" I can be changed by what happens to me, but I refuse to be reduced by it."

—Maya Angelou

CHAPTER 5

THE CHRONIC DISEASE MODEL — THE CASE FOR BIOINTERVENTION

Biointervention is the intervening on a neurological level to help effect positive change in the damaged brain circuitry of a long-time substance abuser. In other words, it is "leveling the playing field."

Addiction could be a natural consequence of humanity's search for the eternal buzz for those who are genetically pre-disposed to the disease. If you resist the premise that there are genetic predispositions to addiction, you will not be able to fully lay the foundation for long lasting recovery. The same way we understand someone's potential to develop diabetes can be seen with addiction. Genetics plays a huge part, but it does not define your outcome. I have seen countless people leading a drug-free life whose whole family was filled with addicted individuals, while I have seen numerous cases of overdose in individuals who have no family history of addiction. It just isn't that simple.

Addiction as a Chronic Disease

Drug addiction is a chronic relapsing disease.[1] Specialists in the field have argued this for a long time. Only in the last 10 years has the greater medical community started to accept this reality. Unfortunately, some individuals in the medical community still perceive addiction as a moral problem, one without biochemical and genetic contributing factors. This lack of understanding complicates and often hinders people's paths toward recovery as well as access to comprehensive care. For this reason, it's more important now than ever to become informed about what is out there and what works and doesn't work for you.

Nearly 50 percent of physicians find it too difficult to talk about addiction with patients.[2] This reality has serious consequences. Unintentionally, we as physicians can contribute indirectly to the problem by prescribing drugs of abuse to patients.

Physicians who refuse to accept that addiction is a chronic, relapsing disease usually have not seen people throughout their life continuum. This has been the gift of being a family doctor. In getting to see people throughout their lives, not just during crises, as many doctors do in other specialties, I have seen how addiction can come and go over a lifespan. It does not mean that other doctors are uninformed, it simply points to the fragmented infrastructure we have in treating disease, and the potential vital role primary care can play in the recovery process.

Understanding addiction as a chronic disease means that we view it the same way we view other chronic diseases such as diabetes and chronic obstructive pulmonary disease (COPD). Consider diabetes, for example, and how we understand it in the context of insulin, insulin receptors, and the use of insulin. Just as we see beta cell dysfunction in the pancreas—and the subsequent treatment of that with insulin—we see a similar picture with addiction and dysfunction in the brain. What we

---

1. JAMA, September 10, 2000 - Volume 290, No. 10.
2. Missed Opportunity: National Survey of Primary Care Physicians and Patients on Substance Abuse, National Center on Addiction and Substance Abuse at Columbia University (CASA). New York, 2000.

have observed is a complete short-circuiting of certain neuro-receptors in PET scans and MRI studies of the brains of individuals that have exhibited long-term abuse of drugs ranging from stimulants such as cocaine or methamphetamines, to alcohol, to opiates such as heroin and their prescription counterparts—opioids[3].

Resistance to the word "disease" is understandable because of its negative connotations. Still, acknowledgment of addiction as a disease allows for the creation of proper treatment plans and leads to the same surveillance and accountability we bring to diabetes and other chronic conditions. It is only with this approach that we see truly effective, long-term outcomes.

Genomic Medicine

We have shed light on the genetic predisposition to addiction through observational studies, but the hard evidence is mounting as well. We have begun isolating the actual genes.

Researchers have studied more than 1,000 peer-reviewed medical publications that linked genes and chromosome regions to drug addiction over the past 30 years and assembled a list of 1,500 addiction-related genes.[4] Scientists around the world have identified hundreds of specific genes that appear to make people more easily addicted to drugs than those without these specific complexes. This discovery opens the door for potentially more effective therapies.

Genetic Heritability – Twin Studies

- Hypertension – 25-50%
- Diabetes – Type 1: 30-55%; Type 2: 80%
- Asthma – 36-70%
- Nicotine – 61% (both sexes)
- Alcohol – 55% (males)
- Marijuana – 52% (females)
- Heroin –34% (males)

McLellan, A.T., et.al., Drug Dependence, a Chronic Medical Illness Journal of the American Medical Association 284:1689-1695, 2000.

3. Am J Psychiatry. 2002 October; 159 (10): 1642-1652.
4. Trends in Neurosciences. Volume 16, Issue 3, March 1993, Pages 83-88.

The more we incorporate real genetic testing and proper family screening into our box of diagnostic tools, the better opportunity we have to tailor treatments for people vulnerable to addiction. By no means does this remove addiction's environmental, behavioral, and psychological roots, but it may allow us to greatly level the playing field to address those influences more effectively now and in the future.

Understanding Your Brain: A Deeper Look at Genetic Susceptibility and Dopamine

Obviously, the brain has many different functions, as seen below.

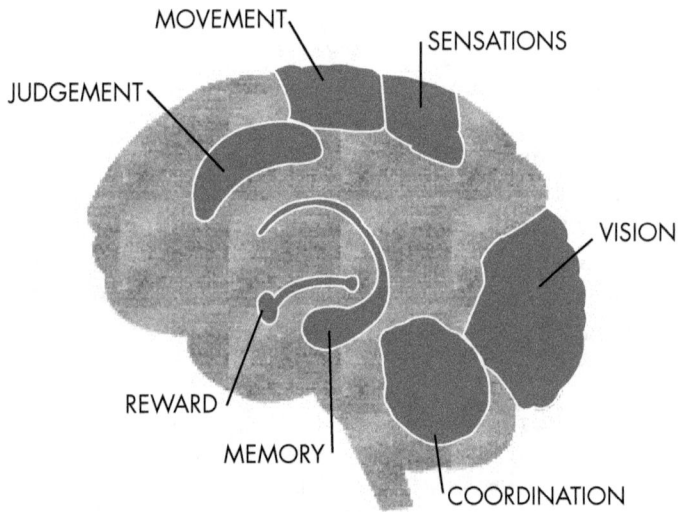

Dopamine is a neurotransmitter associated with movement, attention, learning, and the brain's pleasure and reward system.

Sometimes called "the reward chemical," dopamine gives us the perception of pleasure. It also plays a part in the mesolimbic system, which tells us to eat, drink, go to the bathroom, and have sex—all very primal instincts. Dopamine is essential for the normal functioning of the central nervous system. But it also reinforces the chemical need for continued drug use or abuse.

The limbic system is the part of our brain that is dysfunctional with chronic substance abuse. It could be described as "short-circuited."

Dr. Kenneth Blum, a leading researcher in the field of substance abuse, has been unraveling the link between addiction and genetics for years. He is credited with co-discovering the so-called "alcoholic gene" in 1990. He has since clarified that this gene is more accurately described as the "reward gene."[1]

Several years after discovering the "reward gene," additional studies led Dr. Blum and other researchers to conclude that combinations of genes are probably at play when it comes to addiction. These same genetic markers are also seen in people with compulsive or impulsive disorders, including overeating and obesity, attention deficit disorder, and pathological gambling. To date there are over 2,850 published peer-reviewed articles claiming that the Dopamine D2 receptor gene(s) is associated with addiction and reward dependence behaviors. In short, our genetics tell our dopamine how to behave in our bodies naturally but also how to behave when they are disturbed by drugs or alcohol[2].

Long-term abuse of drugs affects the brain in such a way that it is unable to produce enough dopamine or other neurotransmitters including serotonin, norepinephrine, and other endorphins. When levels of these "feel good" chemicals are low or blocked due to genetic or environmental influences (or due to withdrawal from certain drugs, including alcohol), the results are stress, pain, and restlessness.

---

1. Progress in Brain Research. Cognition, emotion and autonomic responses: The integrative role of the prefrontal cortex and limbic structures. Volume 126, 2000, Pages 325-341.
2. Nature: Neuroscience 8, 1450 - 1457 (2005).

In 1995, Dr. Blum coined the term Reward Deficiency Syndrome. People who suffer from Reward Deficiency Syndrome cannot deal well with stressors, anxiety, pain, or depressive feelings. As a result, they often turn to drugs or alcohol for respite.

Because both genetics and environment affect what Dr. Blum calls the "brain's reward cascade," it is often difficult to determine the root cause of Reward Deficiency Syndrome. However, research indicates that if Reward Deficiency Syndrome has its origins in your genetic makeup, you have the power to change your genes' expression. In fact, his research is a major foundation for the argument of achieving balance through biointervention with amino acid complexes.

Adolescent Drug Abuse

Long-term use or abuse of drugs changes, distorts, and damages the reward system. The prefrontal cortex, a part of the brain that develops during adolescence and into our early 20s, teaches us impulse control. The prefrontal cortex tells us not to jump off a bridge even if all of our friends are doing it. If drug abuse begins during this time, the ability to modulate impulse control, or in other words, to choose between right and wrong, is damaged. Adolescent brains react differently to drugs than adult brains. For this reason, people who have

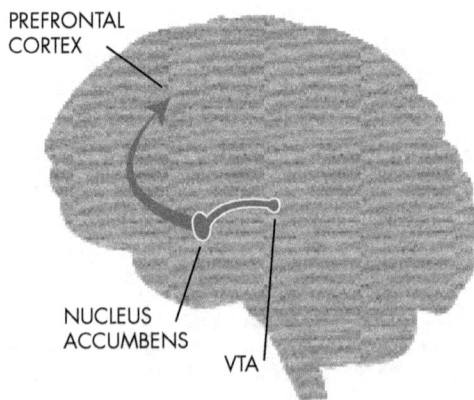

PREFRONTAL CORTEX

NUCLEUS ACCUMBENS

VTA

developed addiction in their younger years have a more challenging prognosis when it comes to recovery.[3] By no means does this imply recovery is hopeless; it simply gives us more information to potentially treat more effectively.

Chronic Care Disease Model of Treatment

If you have been using or abusing drugs for over six to nine months,[4] we now know there are definite changes that have occurred in your brain. Telling someone in this situation to simply stop using is like telling someone to stop eating, drinking, going to the bathroom, or having sex.

Once you make the shift to accepting the chronic disease model, you can make the shift to the chronic disease model of care, which allows for surveillance, safe intervention, goal setting, and continual self-auditing—just like someone with diabetes checking his or her sugar levels.

Thousands of specialists throughout the world agree that addiction is a very difficult condition to treat; but, the greatest numbers of people who create successful recovery do so within this chronic disease model. Therefore, typically if you have been abusing drugs or alcohol for longer than six to nine months, it greatly benefits you to know that there may be actual brain changes that have occurred and to have the humility to accept when the condition demands serious attention. For those of you whose long-term recovery has been elusive, this is not new news. To those of you who are embarking on your recovery strategy for the first time, heed this warning: drug abuse can cause brain damage, and this must be attended to in some fashion.

3. Nature Neuroscience 8, 1429-1430 (2005) doi:10.1038/nn1105-1429
4. Younger, J.W., Chu, L.F., D'Arcy N.T., et al. Prescription opioid analgesics rapidly change the human brain. Pain. Aug 2011; 152(8): 1803-10.

*" If you do what you've
always done, you'll get what
you've always gotten."*

—Anthony Robbins

CHAPTER 6

DETOXIFICATION TO RESTORATION — THE BIOCHEMICAL CONNECTION

Restoration is the repletion or restoring of one's biologic, emotional, psychological, and spiritual self back into balance.

In the prior chapter, we looked at the physiological aspects of addiction. Now let's examine modalities that can help to restore this biochemical imbalance. Each modality has its own distinct level of individual effectiveness. It is important to note again that what works for someone else may not work for you, and vice versa. However, some form of biochemical intervention (biointervention) is usually needed to sustain long-term changes.

You may find that one modality or a combination of modalities is effective. Remember that one size does not fit all; hold on to whatever works for you and let go of whatever doesn't.

Biochemical interventions used to treat addiction include:

– **Exercise**
– **Nutrition**
– **Tailored Nutraceuticals/Amino Acid Therapy**
– **Pharmaceuticals (Medicines)**

They all directly or indirectly address the short-circuiting of the mesolimbic system or malfunctioning of the dopamine system. Interventions can be used by themselves or in conjunction with the others.

Detoxification is usually the first step in the recovery process, but it can take different tacks depending on the severity of an individual's condition.

Restoration of the mesolimbic system can usually happen simultaneously, but takes more time (usually weeks to months) to see the desired effects.

Types of Detoxification

There are three main approaches to detoxification:

Abstinence-based Detoxification

Often, the beginning of abstinence-based treatment includes complete removal of the offending agent(s). People need to completely challenge the use of drugs or medications that they've used illicitly, and sometimes even licitly, usually under the careful watch of an inpatient or outpatient physician. In some cases, people are given psychiatric diagnoses such as depression, anxiety, or bipolar disorder while in the throes of their addiction, or after detoxification. Whenever the assessment is done, there is utility in doing it. Being in the throes of addiction does not preclude an accurate diagnosis of a co-occurring disorder such as depression or anxiety. It may cloud the picture, but it is useful to check[1]. It can help with the overall strategy for recovery after detoxification.

The two main obstacles to abstinence-based treatment are cost and lack of access to care. Because this approach usually demands an inpatient evaluation that goes beyond the 30- or

---

1. Psychiatric Services, 2001. Vol.52, No.5.

60-day model, not everyone can get this level of treatment.

Medication-assisted Detoxification
Some people will utilize medications to help them taper off or stop their drug abuse. This can happen in an inpatient or outpatient setting. When done in an outpatient setting, people will typically only have access to their primary care physicians as well as what the local community may offer in the way of mental health support, such as counseling, family education, social services, group therapies, and community psychiatry. This population is the most susceptible to relapse. Figuring out what works best takes time and needs to happen in a safe and nurturing environment. Those who utilize medication-assisted detoxification in an outpatient setting must have support from others as well as a strong sense of self-motivation. This combination is what supports people to access needed services and create their own safe environment away from negative influences.

Maintenance-assisted Detoxification/Treatment
Some people need a higher level of intervention. Often, these are people who either cannot get themselves into rehab or have been there repeatedly without success. In this case, it is not uncommon for people to use maintenance medicines, such as Methadone or Buprenorphine (for opiate dependence) to work as a bridge. During the process of creating a non-addictive long-term strategy, potentially habit-forming medications may be used, safely in conjunction with a health care provider, to facilitate the unraveling of psychological, emotional, and social challenges. Co-occurring disorders such as depression, anxiety, bipolar disorder, attention deficit disorder, or chronic pain syndromes must be acknowledged and treated at the beginning and during the maintenance phase in order to create a comprehensive long-term recovery plan later.

In complex cases, maintenance medications are used for anywhere from months to a lifetime. In these cases there is a new "normal" and detoxification becomes prolonged—in some cases indefinitely. The illicit substance is removed and replaced with a medication that is potentially just as hazardous or dependence-forming. However, when used correctly, a maintenance medicine can be part of a greater restorative strategy. Recovery does not always mean abstinence from all drugs. Drugs can be tools, dangerous, or both; it depends on the individual and the reason the person is taking the drug.

Biologic Restoration

Amino Acid Therapy

Amino acid therapy is the process of replacing amino acids that have been depleted from the body due to sustained drug use or abuse. Replacing amino acids is often an integral part of the recovery journey. Unless this biochemical deficiency is addressed, most people suffering with addiction are usually faced with continued cravings and relapse[2].

Much data has been collected on the use of amino acids for treatment of addiction. People using amino acid therapy during detoxification and recovery often notice an improvement in their daily lives right away. Often, these amino acids address deficiencies that may have existed before the addiction in the first place. Neurotransmitters have been depleted and amino acids serve as the building blocks to recreate them. One example is N-Acetylcysteine (NAC), an amino acid that may curb cocaine cravings and repair damage in the brain caused by cocaine use. It restores glutamate levels to normal in the area, which ideally decreases cravings. Although not officially approved for cocaine addiction, the off label evidence is promising, and it physiologically makes sense.

There are 20 different kinds of amino acids; some we make in our bodies, others we acquire from our diet. You'll find a variety of amino acid complexes available for purchase, but be sure to exercise caution. Consult with your health care provider before treating yourself via amino acid therapy—especially if you are already on other medicines such as antidepressants, especially MAO inhibitors. Now having seen thousands of patients struggling with addiction, the majority who stay in recovery have maintained a strict hold on their nutrition and nutraceutical regimen.

A nutraceutical is any substance that is a food or a part of a food and provides medical or health benefits.

---

2. J Altern Complement Med. 2000 Feb;6(1):31-5.

Amino Acid Nutrition Therapy

Supplemental Ingredient	Restored Brain Chemical	Addictive Substance Abuse	Amino Acid Deficiency Symptoms	Expected Behavior Change
D-Phenylalanine or DL-Phenylalanine	Enkephalins Endorphins	Heroin, Alcohol, Marijuana, Sweets, Starches, Chocolate, Tobacco	Most Reward Deficiency Syndrome (RDS) conditions sensitive to physical or emotional pain. Crave comfort and pleasure. Desire certain food or drugs.	Reward stimulation. Anti-craving. Mild anti-depression. Mild improved energy and focus. D-Phenylalanine promotes pain relief, increases pleasure.
L-Phenylalanine or L-Tyrosine	Norepinephrine Dopamine	Caffeine, Speed, Cocaine, Marijuana, Aspartame, Chocolate, Alcohol, Tobacco, Sweets, Starches	Most Reward Deficiency Syndrome (RDS) conditions. Depression, low energy. Lack of focus and concentration. Attention-deficit disorder.	Reward stimulation. Anti-craving. Anti-depression. Increased energy. Improved mental focus.
L-Tryptophan or 5 hydroxytryptophan (5HTP)	Serotonin	Sweets, Alcohol, Starch, Ecstasy, Marijuana, Chocolate, Tobacco	Low self-esteem. Obsessive/compulsive behaviors. Irritability or rage. Sleep problems. Afternoon or evening cravings. Negativity. Heat intolerance. Fibromyalgia, SAD (winter blues).	Anti-craving. Anti-depression. Anti-insomnia. Improved appetite control. Improvement in all mood and other serotonin deficiency symptoms.
GABA (Gamma-amino butyric acid)	GABA	Valium, Alcohol, Marijuana, Tobacco, Sweets, Starches	Feeling of being stressed-out. Nervous. Tense muscles. Trouble relaxing.	Promotes calmness. Promotes relaxation.
L-Glutamine	GABA (mild enhancement) Fuel source for entire brain	Sweets, Starches, Alcohol	Stress. Mood swings. Hypoglycemia.	Anti-craving, anti-stress. Levels blood sugar and mood. GABA (mild enhancement). Fuel source for entire brain.

This chart was originally published in the following article:
Blum, K., Ross, J., Reuben, C., Gastelu, D., Miller, D.K. Nutritional Gene Therapy: Natural Healing in Recovery. Counselor Magazine, January/February, 2001.

Nutrition

Proper nutrition is integral to a well-working neurochemical system. A diet rich in fresh fruits, vegetables, lean meats, and whole grains provides the necessary building blocks for the neurotransmitters needed to reach full biochemical restoration. Many people see further success when they supplement their diet with certain nutrients, as well. Equipping your body on a daily basis with essential nutritional "tools" helps diminish cravings while boosting your energy and stamina. Proper nutrition is simply a necessary component of anyone's recovery plan. You may need the assistance of a certified nutritionist to survey your daily eating habits and provide suggestions on how to change them properly and realistically.

To Find a Nutritionist:

You may decide to work directly with a nutritionist. The American Dietetic Association (ADA) web site at eatright.org can help you locate a nutritionist. The ADA is the nation's largest organization of food and nutrition professionals. Their web site provides a "Find a Dietitian" feature locating dietitians in the United States by zip code. Descriptions include areas of practice or specialty for each dietitian.

Although proper nutrition is important, the importance of supplementation cannot be understated in the population suffering with addiction. Depletion of the important building blocks that can be seen with chronic drug or alcohol abuse may need more attention than simply eating more salads and nuts. Proper neurobiological restoration may lay in proper repletion of key nutrients on a daily basis.

Below is a synopsis of the fundamentals when it comes to daily nutritional needs in individuals who have had a history of addiction. It is vital to understand the impact of nutrition on recovery from addiction. Aside from decreased appetite, long standing addiction can lead to gastrointestinal disorders that include the eventual inability to digest properly. This results in specific demands for foods that are high in nutrients to rebuild damaged tissues and organs and to regain proper functioning of the nervous and gastrointestinal systems.

Food affects mood. Proper nutrition actually impacts cravings for drugs and/or alcohol. Long-term addiction creates deficiencies in various amino acids such as tyrosine, glutamine, and tryptophan, and nutrients like B-complex vitamins and folic acid. As building blocks for the production of important neurotransmitters such as norepinephrine, dopamine, and serotonin, decreased levels of these amino acids can negatively affect mood and behavior. This makes the use of drugs and alcohol more attractive, perpetuating a vicious cycle: continued drug use leads to increased malabsorption, which leads to increased nutrient deficiency, which leads back to the need for continued drug use. Therefore, proper supplementation is essential for improved mental clarity, emotional stability, well being, and in this case, long-term recovery. Also, sugar and caffeine intake can add to the overall impact of these imbalances and should be limited to the best of one's ability.

Doses vary and need to be tailored to the individual. Never start any intensive nutrient supplementation without the guidance of your health care provider or nutritionist. Certain medical conditions need to be taken into account before starting a mineral, vitamin, or nutraceutical regimen.

YOURecovery's™ Recommended Daily Supplement Program[1] [2]

---

1. Multivitamin/multimineral supplement – twice a day

2. Probiotics – with every meal

3. Digestive enzymes – after every meal

4. Omega-3 and omega-6 essential fatty acids – 1000-2000 mg three times a day

5. Amino acid complex – once to twice a day

6. Ester C – 1000 mg three times a day

7. B-Complex – 50-100 mg twice a day

8. Calcium/Magnesium 300/150 – twice a day

Exercise

Physical exercise is any bodily activity that enhances or maintains physical fitness and overall health and wellness. Frequent and regular physical exercise boosts the immune system and helps to prevent "diseases of affluence" such as heart disease, cardiovascular disease, type 2 diabetes, and obesity. It also improves mental health, helps to prevent depression, helps to promote or maintain positive self-esteem, and can augment sex appeal or body image.

The road to addiction recovery might start with simply moving your body. The endorphins created by exercise may be the most powerful antidepressants out there and can lay the

---

1. Gant, C. & Lewis, G. (2010). *End Your Addiction Now: The Proven Nutritional Supplement Program That Can Set You Free.* New York: Square One Pub.lishers.
2. Larson, J.M. (1997). *Seven Weeks to Sobriety: The Proven Program to Fight Alcoholism through Nutrition.* New York: Random House.

foundation you need to combat cravings.

A series of studies evaluating the relationship between exercise and substance abuse has produced promising results, prompting the National Institute on Drug Abuse (NIDA) to offer $4 million in grants for additional research into whether regular vigorous activity can prevent addiction.

Restoration as a Continuum
Restoration may be observed on a continuum. Sometimes it's necessary to try different strategies to see what works, either independently or in combination with one another. You may find that by changing your diet and incorporating exercise into your regimen, the "playing field" is leveled but it is the addition of a medicine, vitamin or an extra 15 minutes of daily exercise that pushes you over the hump. You must find your biochemical threshold that leads to optimal recovery.

Consider the way that we treat health issues like high cholesterol. Plenty of people take medication to lower their cholesterol, but this is not a cure-all. They also have a responsibility to change their diet and exercise regimen, reduce stress, and quit smoking. When these environmental factors are ignored, death from heart disease remains a high likelihood.

In other words, the biochemistry may be restored through medication or nutritional intervention, but if you are still continuously exposed to drugs and you have not done any psychological, emotional, social, and spiritual reflection, the biochemical restoration rarely provides long-term rewards.

Pharmaceuticals (Medicines)
A variety of medicines have been approved for treatment of addiction, while others are still in experimental trials. The more common pharmaceuticals are introduced below.

Medication Assistance – Opiate Abuse (Opiate Replacement Therapy)
Physicians will prescribe **buprenorphine** or **methadone** after long-term abuse is seen with opiates such as morphine or heroin, or opioids such as hydrocodone and oxycodone (e.g., Oxycontin™, Percocet™, Vicodin™). So far, opiate

The Restoration Continuum

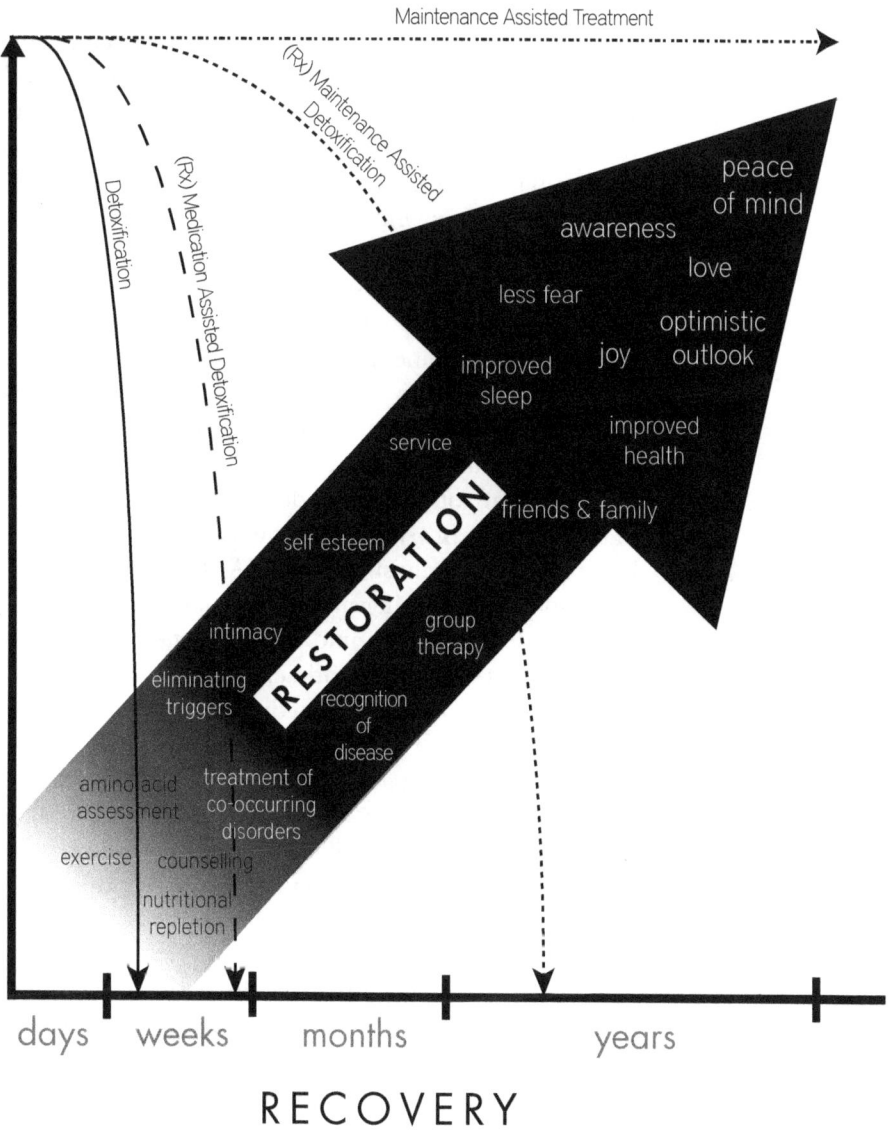

Maintenance Assisted Treatment

(Rx) Maintenance Assisted Detoxification

(Rx) Medication Assisted Detoxification

Detoxification

peace of mind

awareness

love

less fear

optimistic outlook

joy

improved sleep

improved health

service

friends & family

RESTORATION

self esteem

intimacy

group therapy

eliminating triggers

recognition of disease

amino acid assessment

treatment of co-occurring disorders

exercise

counselling

nutritional repletion

days weeks months years

RECOVERY

replacement therapy has the highest success rate for long-term recovery compared to most other treatment plans for opiate abuse.

Buprenorphine is a pain medicine that has been recently approved by the FDA as a new treatment for heroin addiction and other opioid and opiate addictions. It has some major advantages when compared to methadone, including less euphoria (less high), less chance of tolerance, and successful elimination of cravings while paired with psychosocial counseling. Buprenorphine has a ceiling effect on respiratory depression. In other words, it has less of an effect on the breathing center, making it a safer alternative to methadone. Physicians can prescribe buprenorphine in their office, whereas methadone can only be prescribed in state and federally regulated opiate replacement medical centers. Another advantage of buprenorphine, when taken properly, is that it blocks the effects of other opiates that are often abused, decreasing their allure over time. In the U.S., any physician with the required training and Drug Enforcement Administration (DEA) licensing can prescribe buprenorphine (existing in two formulations: Subutex™ and Suboxone™). Keep in mind that physicians who are already certified as psychiatrists or addiction specialists are often more skilled in administering this medicine.

Methadone is a long acting opiate that, when taken properly, can significantly reduce opiate craving and ideally block the effect of illegal opiates. Acquiring the medicine requires frequent visits to a state and federally regulated clinic. View a list of these clinics at www.atforum.com.

While logistically difficult to acquire, methadone saves thousands of lives every year and remains the most effective primary treatment according to the National Institute of Health (NIH) for opiate abuse. In November of 1997, the NIH heard testimony from 25 experts that reviewed 941 research reports published from January 1994 - September 1997. This was their consensus:

"Of the various treatments available, MMT (Methadone Maintenance Treatment), combined with attention to medical, psychiatric, and socioeconomic issues, as well as drug counseling, has the highest probability of being effective."[3]

Caution is strongly advised with people who take methadone while still abusing opiates or alcohol, as additive effects can lead to respiratory failure and death. Any medicine used under the umbrella of opiate replacement therapy is maximized with psycho-social-emotional intervention, whether in the form of individual counseling, group therapy, or treatment of co-occurring disorders. Methadone or buprenorphine used by itself without any other intervention is incomplete, usually ineffective long-term, and loses sight of the potential biochemical repair that is needed in most cases. If you are doing a maintenance program, get busy! You should fill your recovery tool kit with the interpersonal tools needed for long-term recovery during this time of medication-induced stability. Relapse awaits those who detoxify before their "ducks are in a row" (restoratively, psychologically, socially, emotionally, and spiritually).

Utilizing this medicine is important for weeks to months and even years in some individuals before detoxification is a good plan for long-term success. Physical withdrawal from buprenorphine or methadone is not severe when the medicine is tapered slowly. However, there may be long-term side effects, including fatigue, bowel disorders, and mood disturbances such as increased depression and anxiety, just as is seen with illicit opiate abuse. It is therefore all the more important to lay the groundwork in advance by assessing and treating potential co-occurring disorders; tailoring nutraceuticals or nutritional therapy; engaging in counseling; cultivating a supportive, pro-recovery environment; and adhering to an exercise plan.

Medication Assistance – Alcohol Abuse
Acamprosate, also commonly known as Campral™, lowers the chance of relapse by reducing the cravings that result when abstaining from alcohol. Widely used in Europe to reduce alcohol cravings in drinkers who have quit, acamprosate was approved by the FDA after studies showed that more subjects given the drug abstained from alcohol compared with those who were given a placebo. However, the FDA cautions

---

3. National Institute of Health, November 1997.

that acamprosate might not be effective for people who are currently drinking when they start the medicine or for those who are misusing other substances. Some studies have shown acamprosate to be more effective in type 2 alcoholism, usually found in individuals who have a strong family history of alcohol abuse.

Disulfiram, also commonly known as Antabuse™, is one of the oldest medicines approved for treatment of alcohol dependence. In use since 1951, it is what is known as an aversive agent, producing a feeling of nausea when alcohol is consumed. Additional side effects include flushing, headache, vomiting, dizziness, and lowered blood pressure. Disulfiram can be added to other medicines or used by itself. There is a population that can continue to drink on disulfiram, suggesting that their addiction is so severe that they can withstand the side effects. Using disulfiram with alcohol can create a dangerous combination, requiring careful surveillance by a health care provider. In some cases, disulfiram is very successful when used in conjunction with counseling and group therapies.

Recent research suggests that disulfiram is effective in reducing cocaine abuse, especially in conjunction with cognitive behavioral therapy.

Naltrexone is a medicine prescribed to treat alcohol abuse as well as opiate abuse. Naltrexone lessens the euphoric effect by blocking the parts of the brain that feel pleasure when using alcohol or opiates.

Naltrexone has been shown to improve treatment outcomes in people addicted to alcohol or opiates by decreasing cravings when combined with other interventions, such as Alcoholics Anonymous or Narcotics Anonymous meetings, addiction counseling, family therapy, group therapy, and hospital or residential treatment.

Medication Assistance – Stimulant Abuse
No medications exist that are directly indicated for actual stimulant abuse. Stimulants include cocaine, methamphetamines, and prescription stimulant medicines. However, many medications are used off label, or not as indicated, to repair

the biochemistry that has been short-circuited from stimulant abuse.

Gabapentin and **vigabatrin** (only approved in Canada) are different medications with similar effects. Both have been used off label for cocaine cravings. They are anticonvulsants, which ideally reduce cocaine use, make cravings easier to overcome, and cause relapses to be less severe. Both work by increasing the GABA, a neurotransmitter, in an individual's brain and may cause sedation.

Baclofen is a muscle relaxant that has been found to curb cocaine cravings and reduce use of cocaine, especially in chronic, heavy users. It can increase the neurotransmitter GABA, like gabapentin, and has been used off label in cocaine addiction.

Nocaine provides a weaker version of cocaine's effects, and can, under medical supervision, block the stimulant effects of cocaine. This is similar to methadone maintenance therapy, but for stimulants instead of opiates.

Modafinil promotes longer total sleep time and decreases daytime sleepiness in abstinent cocaine users. This medicine has been shown off label to be useful in an overall recovery plan that includes cognitive behavioral therapy for cocaine addiction. Researchers are not entirely sure how it works, but modafinil may increase the release of dopamine in the brain's reward center.

What to Look For in an Addiction Medicine Specialist

An addiction medicine specialist, or addictionologist, should never be stuck on dogma, but rather be driven by outcomes. Seek out a specialist who acts as your steward, someone who offers evidence-based strategies as well as sincere concern for the severity of your addiction at any moment of any given day. If you acknowledge that you have tried medicine, rehab, and group therapy, but the only thing that keeps you from drinking is church, or your divorce, or your relationship with your son, then your physician should accept that fact and officially incorporate it into your medical chart and your personal recovery tool kit. A good addiction medicine specialist

Prescribing legal drugs to combat addiction is complicated. Each person's situation is unique and this must be taken into account. Consider the following example.

Q. Can I use Ritalin™ or Adderall™ (both stimulant medications) to treat my attention deficit disorder (ADD) if I have a cocaine/stimulant addiction?

It depends on the individual. The answer is yes if you are using cocaine to cope with ADD and establish continued functionality in your workplace and relationships. Using a prescribed stimulant could challenge and ideally stabilize the pattern of increasing cocaine use, eventually leading to its discontinuation. Of course, you would need to show no sign of prescribed stimulant abuse.

The answer is no if, instead of properly using the prescribed stimulant, you abuse it or mix it with cocaine and snort the whole batch in one night. This is simply one example of many that could reflect abuse of a prescribed medication.

will endorse strategies that work for you, not only what may appear to work on paper. Your recovery is unique to you, and you must find someone who understands that.

Medications vs. No Medications

Is there such a thing as medication-assisted sobriety? This is an easy answer for those who practice addiction medicine. It's not about someone else's definition of sobriety, it is about Your Recovery! Any treatment decision needs to reflect your history with addiction, family history, social situation/support, potential co-occurring mental health diagnosis, other medical conditions, history of treatment, and readiness to make changes. Therefore, the answer is yes, as long as you challenge the definitions of "clean" and "sober." These words hold different meanings to different people; find a definition that makes sense to you.

What follows is a story that I hear again and again—sadly, it is at the expense of a successful recovery strategy.

Your sponsor at AA says that you should not be using your medicine for depression because "then you're never really clean." Your doctor recommends two more medicines, one of which could potentially be abused, and tells you that your sponsor is not being helpful. Where do you turn? Who do you trust?

This situation highlights the importance of knowing your personal recovery goals and finding a support team that understands your path to recovery is unique. When people are given contradictory advice, the outcomes are very poor, and too often include overdose and death.

A Note about Chronic Pain and Addiction

Opioids are medications derived from the poppy plant, which is also used to produce opium, morphine, and heroin. Opioids such as hydrocodone and oxycodone have relieved millions of the acute or chronic pain they've suffered with for years.

I have patients who take opioids three times a day for their chronic pain. And I have patients for whom this would be a terrible strategy—even though they have the same pain diagnosis. The difference lies in the patients' relationship with these medications, their genetic makeup, their personal history of addiction, their social environment, as well as their current psychological and psychiatric state. All of these factors are crucial in determining the best approach regarding medications like hydrocodone and oxycodone that are potentially addicting.

Chronic pain and addiction present unique challenges that often need careful teamwork by a good pain physician, addiction medicine specialist, and primary care provider. People in this situation must be willing to explore alternative solutions like acupuncture, pain psychology, massage, yoga, and physical therapy. Two excellent resources for this population are Pain Recovery by Dr. Mel Pohl and The Gift of Pain by Paul Brand and Philip Yancey.

" Fall seven times, stand up
eight."

—Japanese proverb

CHAPTER 7

RELAPSE AND
CO-OCCURRING DISORDERS

People utilize different modalities throughout their lives to maintain lifelong recovery. But the reality is that people do relapse, even with the use of multiple conventional and alternative strategies.

If you survive a relapse, it can be a fantastic opportunity to learn about your triggers. Reflect on the instigating factor that contributed to the relapse after a period of sobriety. Your goal should be to manage a relapse in a continual learning mode, devoid of shame and embarrassment.

Life is still challenging even when you have your three core recovery components in place, but specific challenges may reveal roots of the initial allure of drugs. For this reason, it's imperative to have a defined recovery strategy and a healthy acceptance of what does and doesn't work for you. Know when to add, subtract, or combine different strategies. Don't beat yourself up if acupuncture works for your friend while it doesn't work for you.

If recovery remains elusive, even with the best attempts conventionally as well as alternatively, you must look at what lies beneath the surface. It's quite possible that you are experiencing a co-occurring issue that could actually be the primary reason for your addiction in the first place.

Co-Occurring Disorders and Addiction

All of us have had feelings of sadness. All of us have experienced anxiety. All of us have perceived some level of trauma, whether psychological or physical. The key is to determine whether these feelings are symptomatic of an actual disease or disorder and whether they have caused you to become addicted to drugs. The Diagnostic and Statistical Manual of Mental Disorders, Fourth Edition (DSM-IV) does its best to articulate the differences between simply feeling lousy and actual disease. But the best way to determine whether you may be suffering with an additional disease beyond addiction may be to ask yourself, quite simply, whether these feelings are causing your life to be dysfunctional. Are they causing a problem?

Recognizing the potential for co-occurring disorders with addiction is imperative. In fact, it is estimated that somewhere between 30 and 70 percent of people who suffer with addiction also suffer with another disorder.[1] In order to achieve recovery, you must become aware of any co-occurring disorders and treat them as you are treating your addiction.

Let's use depression as an example. Many people believe that the best "medicines" to treat their depression are drugs and/or alcohol. For some, "self-medicating" leads to addiction. This population faces two separate medical conditions—addiction and depression—both of which need attention, treatment, and strategies for healing. If one issue is attended to and one is ignored, the result is incomplete treatment.

Often, the co-occurring disorders seen with addiction are depression, panic and anxiety disorders, post traumatic stress disorder (PTSD), attention deficit disorder, and mood disorders (bipolar disorders).

1. Aronoff, 2000; Heit, 2004; Christensen, 2006; Porter, 1980.

The DSM-IV (or simply DSM) is the current reference used by mental health professionals and physicians to diagnose mental disorders. The American Psychiatric Association (APA) began publishing the DSM in 1952, and it has since been through several revisions. The latest edition was published in 2000 and an updated edition is expected in 2012. The current DSM lists over 200 mental health conditions and the criteria required for each one in making an appropriate diagnosis.

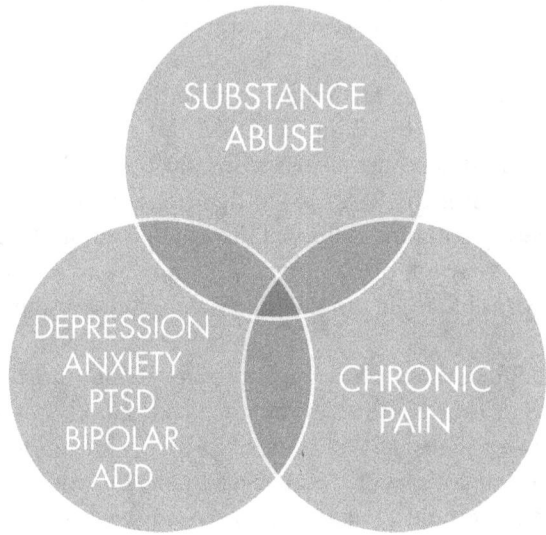

The need to isolate, understand, and ideally treat a potential co-occurring condition is invaluable to your overall recovery process. If you fail to do this, you'll be taking two steps forward and one step back throughout recovery. Again, keep in mind that it is these co-occurring conditions that may set people up for addiction in the first place.

If you believe you may be suffering with a co-occurring disorder, see a qualified professional who can help you make an accurate diagnosis using clinical judgment and experience. Self-diagnosis is not always a good idea and may lead to ineffective and even risky treatment decisions.

Putting It All Together

Consider these three stories that share both commonalities

and differences.

Mark

Mark struggled with alcohol dependence for most of his 46 years. It was not until he started regularly attending AA, changed his diet significantly, got out of his dysfunctional relationship with his partner, and finally began writing the book that he always wanted to, that he was able to find long-lasting sobriety.

Tina

Tina struggled with alcohol dependence for most of her 46 years. It was not until she started taking medicine for her depression, prioritized quality time with her family, and began exercising every morning that she was able to find long-lasting sobriety.

Greg

Greg struggled with alcohol dependence for most of his 46 years. It was not until he entered detox and rehab for 60 days, utilized intensive individual therapy, amino acids and nutraceuticals for his co-occurring anxiety from childhood trauma, and accepted the support from his grown children, that he was able to find long-lasting sobriety.

Mark, Tina, and Greg have much in common—in addition to alcohol ruling their lives, they were the same age and came from similar backgrounds. Their differences lie in what finally worked to keep them on track with their sobriety. Each recovery strategy was unique, and yet each was just as effective.

Recovery demands an investigation of yourself and a freeing of barriers obstructing your personal journey towards sobriety. Figure out what works for you, commit to your strategy, and challenge your preexisting belief systems if they stand in the way of a better life.

> *" Our greatest weakness lies in giving up. The most certain way to succeed is always to try just one more time."*
>
> *—Thomas Edison*

UNIT 3

YOURECOVERY™ TOOL KIT
"FILLING IN THE HOLES"

Once you have created the foundation for your recovery story and given good attention to the three essential components, it is usually time to fill in the "holes." By now you should be very familiar with those three core elements. They are:

YOUR PURPOSE. That which is your main motivation for seeking long-term recovery. Be specific.

INTERPERSONAL INTERVENTION. Reconnection. The nurturing of the important relationships that will be vital to your recovery success, and the developing of effective long lasting tools, usually with a counselor or psychologist.

BIOINTERVENTION. The way you have leveled the playing field biochemically—whether through medicines, nutraceuticals, exercise, and/or nutrition; this includes treatment of any co-occurring mental health conditions (e.g., depression, anxiety, ADD).

I can't overemphasize the importance of keeping an open mind during this part of the recovery process. Long-term recovery usually requires thinking outside the box. If these three core elements were all people needed, we would have a cure already. These three core elements lay the foundation for long-term success. Evidence exists to support diverse healing modalities from all over the world, many of which are thousands of years older than conventional medicine. Dare yourself to explore your options and perhaps take a leap of faith to "fill in the holes." Remember, everyone's success story is a bit different, and we often need to build on this foundation to sustain long-term recovery.

" If opportunity doesn't knock, build a door."

– Milton Berle

CHAPTER 8

THE TOOLS: YOUR A - Z INTEGRATIVE GUIDE

Real long-term recovery demands openness to complementary and alternative modalities as well as conventional medicine and its elements of surveillance and intervention. It demands a true integrative, or holistic, approach that takes into account the whole person, not just the addiction. The following is not a comprehensive list of modalities, but rather a selection of the most common, evidence-based, and effective ones in people's individualized long-term recovery plans. This list is meant to give you an idea of the multitude of tools that can be used to give meaning and details to YOUR three core elements. These are methods you can use to build on that foundation and to push survival and transient recovery into recovery solutions that last a lifetime.

Acupuncture and Chinese Medicine
Chinese medicine, which includes acupuncture as an integral intervention, has been providing tools to people suffering with addiction for thousands of years. Chinese medical theory is based on the concept of yin and yang. These concepts reflect the opposites observed in all the processes of nature, including the "addicted brain." In a healthy individual, yin and yang are in relative balance, but in individuals suffering with addiction, there is often a deficiency in the yin. Acupuncture has been used in the detoxification process with much success, and is

often utilized throughout a person's recovery journey.

The first acupuncture detoxification clinic in the United States opened in 1974 at the Lincoln Memorial Hospital in the South Bronx neighborhood of New York City.

Initially, acupuncture was used as an adjunct to methadone treatment in opiate dependent individuals, but the acupuncture results were so promising that methadone was dropped from the program. People who use acupuncture report decreased cravings, withdrawal relief, and all-around improvement of their well being. Currently, public-funded acupuncture detoxification programs exist throughout the country.

Acupuncture typically involves nourishing the yin by treating points on the outside of the ear. Short, thin, sterile needles are inserted at three to five points. Treatment is usually tailored to the individual, not the addiction, and frequency ranges from daily to periodically throughout a person's life. Acupuncture and Chinese medicine can be either a complementary or an integral part of an individual's recovery tool box.

Amino Acid Therapy
Amino acids, often utilized in some combination via various nutraceutical companies, are an important support piece when it comes to the restoration process. When using amino acid therapy, people often see many of their emotional and psychological challenges lessened, if not rebalanced, as well as a renewed desire to engage in therapy and other recovery pursuits.

Some people interested in amino acid therapy work directly with a nutritionist, or dietitian. The American Dietetic Association (ADA) is the nation's largest organization of food and nutrition professionals. Their website (eatright.org) can help you locate a nutritionist in your area.

See chapter 6 for more information about amino acid therapy.

Aromatherapy
Aromatherapy uses essential oils extracted from plants and herbs that can be inhaled or applied to the skin. Aromas

derived from these natural plant sources have been shown to produce positive effects on the mind and the body in clinical studies. As an adjunct to one's recovery strategy, aromatherapy helps with stress reduction.

Check out Aroma Web (aromaweb.com) for more information about aromatherapy.

Art Therapy

Art has an inherent ability to connect people with their emotions. The American Art Therapy Association (AATA) defines art therapy as a modality "that utilizes art media, images, the creative art process, and patient/client responses to the created products as reflections of an individual's development, abilities, personality, interests, concerns, and conflicts."

Trauma, family struggles, or other issues may make communicating with a therapist challenging. The opportunity to communicate in a nonverbal, non-threatening way through drawing, painting, sculpting, photography, or other forms of art allows for breakthroughs and ideally, strategies to maintain recovery.

Because art therapy doesn't feel like therapy, people are often highly receptive to this form of self-exploration. Rather than sitting down and saying, "Let's talk about you," art therapists can focus on the individual's artistic creation as a means of starting a dialogue about difficult memories and emotions.

Animal Therapy

Interactions with animals have long been known to provide a very therapeutic experience—both physiologically and psychologically. Animal therapy has been used in a wide variety of settings to help people with chemical dependency. Often, people who engage in animal therapy report decreased stress levels; reduced feelings of anger and anxiety; improved social functioning; and increased feelings of trust, patience, and self-esteem.

The following are residential treatment centers that offer equine (horse) therapy:
Sierra Tucson (sierratucson.com)

Cirque Lodge (cirquelodge.com)
Cottonwood (cottonwooddetucson.com)
English Mountain Recovery (emrecovery.org)

Ayurvedic Medicine

Ayurveda is a Sanskrit word meaning "life science." Originating in India in 7 or 8 BC, Ayurvedic medicine is a system of preventive health care. According to Ayurveda, health is based on the harmonious relationship between three biological principles called doshas: Vata (air), Pitta (fire), and Kapha (water). Ayurveda includes diet and herbal remedies and places equal emphasis on body, mind, and spirit in disease prevention and treatment. An Ayurvedic practitioner provides tools to the individual to rebalance his/her doshas, thereby supporting overall recovery. Many people have found long-term answers for their addictions working with an Ayurvedic practitioner.

Biofeedback

Biofeedback is a scientific way to learn about your own stress and create strategies to reduce it. Biofeedback practitioners use instruments that provide immediate knowledge about the level of tension in the body. People practicing biofeedback often feel they've gained invaluable tools in learning how to control their own physiology.

Learning how to reduce tension and stress is integral to a long-term recovery strategy, especially because stress may have led to use or abuse of drugs in the first place. Assessing your own level of stress, or the triggers that cause stress, allows you to implement stress reduction strategies preventively or proactively.

Body Work

Often, the onset of chronic pain conditions leads people to addiction innocently. For those predisposed to addiction, conventional medical strategies that utilize potentially addictive substances can create additional problems. In this population, non-pharmaceutical options are imperative in order to create long-term solutions for chronic pain.

Medical Massage

Medical massage is outcome-based massage. In other words,

concrete goals are created via the manipulation of the muscles as to create proper functioning and pain reduction. It is primarily the application of specific treatment protocols targeted to the patient's problem(s), as diagnosed by a physician. The treatment is administered after a thorough assessment by the medical massage therapist. Medical massage therapists have extensive training in anatomy, as well as pathology (disease) and recovery from injury. Medical massage therapy focuses on assisting the body in its natural healing processes. Specialized modalities such as cranial sacral, myofascial, lymphatic, and neuromuscular fall into the category of medical massage.

Swedish Massage

Swedish massage is one of the most common forms of massage therapy. It is a relaxing and therapeutic form of body work. Originating in Europe, this type of massage manipulates the muscles with the use of oils and different kinds of movements, including long strokes, kneading, and tapping. It is used to increase circulation and flexibility, soothe muscles, and reduce tension. Swedish massage is often essential in the individual who needs to "de-stress" as part of their overall recovery strategy

Rolfing™

Rolfing™, also known as structural integration, is the system of body work founded by Dr. Ida Pauline Rolf. This body work technique involves deep massaging of the connective tissues that envelop the muscles and organs. The aim of Rolfing™ is to ensure that all bones, tissues, and organs are in their correct position in the body. Benefits of Rolfing™ are said to include improvement in balance and flexibility, stress relief, and higher energy levels.

Chiropractic Medicine

"Chiropractics" comes from Greek and means "done by hand." It is grounded in the principle that the body can heal itself when the skeletal system is correctly aligned and the nervous system is functioning properly. To achieve this, the practitioner uses his/her hands or an adjusting tool to perform specific manipulations of the vertebrae. If vertebrae are out of place, or "subluxated," the theory is that nerve transmission is disrupted and causes pain in the back as well as other areas of the body. Chiropractic medicine has helped countless people who suffer with chronic pain but need to avoid potentially habit-forming or abused pain medications.

Energy Medicine

Energy medicine is based upon the belief that changes in the "life force" of the body, including the electric, magnetic, and electromagnetic fields, affect human health and can promote healing. Among people looking for alternative modalities to treat their pain in the context of addiction, energy medicine has long been a vital component to recovery.

Therapeutic Touch

Therapeutic touch (TT), also called non-contact therapeutic touch (NCTT), healing touch, or distance healing, is an energy therapy that promotes healing while reducing pain and anxiety. Practitioners of Therapeutic Touch place their hands on, or near, a patient, to detect and manipulate the patient's energy field. The following two sites are helpful in locating a TT practitioner:

www.healingtouchinternational.org
www.healingtouchprogram.com

Reiki

Reiki is a Japanese form of complementary and alternative medicine, developed (or rediscovered) during the latter half of the 19th century. Reiki comes from the Japanese word meaning "universal life force energy." The practitioner serves as a conduit for healing energy directed into the recipient's body or energy field without physical contact. Reiki has been used in addiction treatment for decades and has been a valuable adjunct to many people's overall recovery strategy.

Environmental Medicine

Environmental medicine, or toxicology, is a multidisciplinary field involving medicine, environmental science, and chemistry, among others. It may be viewed as the medical branch of the broader field of environmental health. Environmental medicine involves studying the interactions between environment and human health as well as the role of the environment in causing disease.

Environmental factors that cause disease can be found in the physical, chemical, and biological world. Some people, for example, may manifest mental disorders, such as anxiety or depression, from exposure to an environmental toxin. This mental disorder may then predispose them to addiction. Environmental medicine seeks to remove the offending toxins—in other words, it seeks to treat the cause, not the symptom.

Exercise

Physical exercise is any bodily activity that enhances or maintains physical fitness and overall health and wellness. Frequent and regular physical exercise boosts the immune system and helps to prevent "diseases of affluence" such as heart disease, cardiovascular disease, type 2 diabetes and obesity. It also improves mental health, helps to prevent depression, helps to promote or maintain positive self-esteem, and can augment sex appeal or body image. Probably most importantly, it helps to boost the often depleted neurotransmitters seen in long-term drug or alcohol abuse.

See chapter 6 for more information about exercise.

Facilitated Breathwork and Abdominal Breathing

"Breathwork" refers to many forms of the conscious alteration of breathing, such as hyperventilation or connecting the inhalation and exhalation, when used within psychotherapy or meditation. Proponents believe the technique may be used to attain different levels of consciousness and that the practice of breathwork techniques may produce spiritual or psychological benefits. When the modern breath-oriented therapies were first developed in the 1970s, they were often influenced by ideas from psychotherapy.

"Mindfulness of breathing" or "conscious breathing" can be done alone or led by a facilitator who guides the patient through a host of different breathing sessions.

Genetic Testing

Addiction, like other chronic disease states, is supported by consistent emerging data indicating its genetic origins. Although we are inevitably shaped by our personality, culture, and environment, genetics may play a bigger role than we once believed. Sometimes, the knowledge gained through genetic testing can help direct more focused treatment.

Group Therapies

Group therapy is a type of psychotherapy that involves two or more individuals who work with one or a group of counselors or therapists. This modality is a common ally of people recovering from addiction. Group therapy is popular among support groups, where participating group members can share, learn from the experiences of others, and give advice. Group therapy can be defined in many ways. It includes 12-step programs, spirituality- or religion-based groups, family therapy or simply talk therapy in a group session. Recovery tools can be obtained in group settings via listening or sharing experiences. For many people, group therapy is integral to their daily recovery.

The Twelve Steps

(Reprinted from The Big Book, *AA Worldwide Services, 1939)*

Step 1 - We admitted we were powerless over drugs and/or alcohol—that our lives had become unmanageable.

Step 2 - Came to believe that a Power greater than ourselves could restore us to sanity.

Step 3 - Made a decision to turn our will and our lives over to the care of God as we understood Him.

Step 4 - Made a searching and fearless moral inventory of ourselves.

Step 5 - Admitted to God, to ourselves, and to another human being the exact nature of our wrongs.

Step 6 - Were entirely ready to have God remove all these defects of character.

Step 7 - Humbly asked Him to remove our shortcomings.

Step 8 - Made a list of all persons we had harmed, and became willing to make amends to them all.

Step 9 - Made direct amends to such people wherever possible, except when to do so would injure them or others.

Step 10 - Continued to take personal inventory and when we were wrong promptly admitted it.

Step 11 - Sought through prayer and meditation to improve our conscious contact with God as we understood Him, praying only for knowledge of His Will for us and the power to carry that out.

Step 12 - Having had a spiritual awakening as the result of these steps, we tried to carry this message to alcoholics, and to practice these principles in all our affairs.

Remember that god means many things to different people. If it bothers you, replace the word "God" with cosmic consciousness, nature, the soul, or our general inter-connectedness. Too many people have lost access to this great tool due to cultural or spiritual differences. Don't let language get in the way of your recovery. Groups are usually free, safe, and are filled with people that share common goals. You share only what you want to share. The 12 steps act as a guidepost to millions of people every day.

Homeopathy

Homeopathy is a form of alternative medicine in which practitioners treat patients using highly diluted preparations of different substances. The premise is this: the more dilute a substance, the greater its ability to reproduce symptoms of a particular ailment, and hence activate the body's own immune system to counter and "fight" the disease.

The regulation and prevalence of homeopathy is highly variable from country to country. There are no legal regulations concerning its use in some countries, while in others, licenses in conventional medicine from accredited universities are required.

Research is currently being undertaken to understand how and why these remedies work on the mental and physical level. Specific homeopathic remedies may be helpful during the period of withdrawal from alcohol or drugs, during detoxification, and as part of a maintenance plan for long-term recovery.

Hyperbaric Oxygen Therapy

Hyperbaric oxygen therapy (HBOT), also known as hyperbaric medicine, is the medical use of oxygen at a level higher than atmospheric pressure. The premise is that the more oxygen that gets to one's tissues, the greater chance for self-healing.

Currently approved in the United States to treat pathological conditions such as decompression sickness, air embolisms, gas gangrene, and carbon monoxide poisoning, HBOT has also been used to treat more unconventional ailments such as autism, cerebral palsy, hearing loss, traumatic brain injury and multiple sclerosis. Medical complications relating to misuse of HBOT include potential pressure damage to various organs of the body. Still, HBOT as treatment for devastating diseases continues to be explored.

The use of HBOT in addiction is being researched and utilized in many clinics around the U.S. as well as internationally. Data is mixed on its results, but for some, it has been a vital component of their recovery.

Hypnosis

Usually delivered by a "hypnotist" or self-administered, hypnosis is commonly composed of a long series of preliminary instructions and suggestions that can tap into a person's subconscious. Suggestions are then given in a hypnotized state, allowing people to "let go of" or process painful or unnecessary thought patterns. The use of hypnotism for therapeutic purposes is referred to as "hypnotherapy."

Recent research suggests that although hypnotic subjects are fully awake during a session, there is an increased response to suggestions. When hypnotized, the mind is especially receptive to ideas and suggestions. Specific goals can be articulated before a session, and many people have found hypnosis to be a very useful part of a total recovery program.

101

Imagery

Imagery, or guided visualization, is a technique using positive thoughts and images to relieve pain, calm an individual down, and stimulate overall healing. It is a relaxation technique in which a person visualizes or imagines things suggested to them by a recording or counselor. Often people in recovery use guided imagery or visualization techniques daily to aid in their overall recovery process.

Life Coaching

Life coaches are individuals with a background in sociology or psychology who are dedicated to helping people achieve their life goals by developing their decision-making skills, as well as short- and long-term strategies. Sometimes considered more pragmatic than individual counseling, a life coach often helps people create their day-in and day-out strategies for reaching their life goals. In recovery, having a life coach on your team can provide much needed assistance with the "new life" recovery brings.

Meditation

Meditation is a holistic discipline in which the practitioner attempts to get beyond the reflexive, "thinking" mind into a deeper state of relaxation or awareness. Meditation is a component of many religions and has been practiced since antiquity. There are many different kinds of meditation, including transcendental, Zen, and guided. Meditation is a very valuable tool to those who are able to practice it, especially in terms of its utility as a recovery tool. Often, meditation allows people the time and insight to take a mental inventory of what is in their recovery tool box and consider how those tools can be used on a day-to-day basis.

Music Therapy

Music therapy has many different definitions, but the main goal resides in the use of different melodies to provide restoration of health and improve overall well-being. The implementation of music therapy involves interactions of the therapist, client, and music. As the musical components of rhythm, melody and harmony are played out, the therapist and client can develop relationships which maximize the client's quality of life. In recovery from addiction, accessing the senses, especially hearing, can provide valuable insight into a person's needs when it comes to stress reduction and overall healing.

(Based on the definition of music therapy in the Joint Declaration of the 1982 International Symposium of Music Therapists)

Nature Medicine

Nature medicine, also known as wilderness therapy or eco-intervention, is used in countless inpatient treatment centers. The power of complete immersion in nature is grounding for many people. Whether it is the reliability of lapping ocean waves or the tranquility of a mountain lake, nature offers people in recovery a source of stability—an anchor of sorts.
Often, during the recovery process, one must establish a deeper connection with others and the surrounding natural world. Trust in one's belonging to this planet can serve as a reminder that one is part of something greater than oneself. People who spend time reconnecting with the natural world can "summon" it as a kind of armor against life's "curve balls."

Naturopathic Medicine

Naturopathic medicine is a distinct system of primary health care—an art, science, philosophy, and practice of diagnosis, treatment, and prevention of illness. Naturopathic physicians are primary health care practitioners whose diverse techniques include modern and traditional, scientific and empirical methods.

Naturopaths are like primary care physicians. They help people move through their addictions and other chronic or acute medical conditions and continually oversee the recovery process in a holistic way. Like allopathic or osteopathic doctors (M.D.s and D.O.s), they practice an evidence-based model of medicine that is based on the objective observation of nature and how it affects the human condition. There is an emphasis on absorption and gut, or gastrointestinal, health as a vital component to recovery and overall wellness.

Naturopaths differ from primary care physicians in regard to their training with emergency and surgical procedures and the prescribing of medications. Otherwise, naturopathic physicians that work closely with M.D.s and D.O.s can provide people with a team-oriented, forward-thinking medical safety net that optimizes biochemical restoration at its roots.

Nutraceuticals
Nutraceuticals — "Food, or parts of food, that provide medical or health benefits, including the prevention and treatment of disease." –Dr. Stephen DeFelice, Foundation for Innovation in Medicine

Proper nutrition is integral to any successful long-term recovery plan. Only by obtaining the essential nutrients can your body begin to rebuild the neurolimbic system that has been damaged during a long stint with substance abuse.
B-vitamins and good pharmaceutical-grade fish oils are a staple in most recovery strategies. Both carry essential nutrients that have to be repleted (replaced) often daily for long periods of time to get their maximal effect. But the people that stick with it have a clear and distinct advantage over the people that do not. This is seen in mood, joint health, and energy, as well as an overall sense of well-being. It is important to tailor nutritional needs to the individual—not just the addiction.

See chapter 6 for more information about nutraceuticals.

Osteopathic Medicine
Doctors of osteopathic medicine (D.O.) complete a course of study equivalent to that of an M.D. at an osteopathic medical school. They are trained in the awareness of the effects of body mechanics on health and disease processes. Osteopaths are licensed to practice medicine and surgery just as medical doctors are; in addition, they often use manipulation techniques similar to chiropractors or physical therapists.

See "Tenets of Osteopathic Medicine" in the Note from the Author section for more information.

Pharmaceuticals (Medicines)
See chapter 6 for more information about pharmaceuticals.

Some good websites that can help people navigate the numerous medications available for addiction, from heroin and prescription pain pills to tobacco and alcohol abuse, include:

Substance Abuse & Mental Health Services Administration (SAMHSA)
www.samhsa.gov

Medical Assisted Treatment of America
www.medicalassistedtreatment.org

Medical Assisted Treatment of America is a national organization that was founded by advocates for the medical treatment of addiction. It supports the idea of addiction as a medical illness rather than a social ill and acts as a mediator for patients to ensure that quality treatment is available. The website provides a great deal of information on opiate drug treatment, patients' rights, methadone maintenance, legal issues, and addiction science.

National Alliance of Advocates for Buprenorphine Treatment (NAABT)
www.naabt.org

The NAABT is a non-profit organization dedicated to educating the public about opioid addiction and buprenorphine treatment, helping to reduce the stigma associated with addiction, and connecting patients with qualified treatment providers. The website includes a buprenorphine treatment locator and educational information.

Suboxone Assisted Treatment
www.suboxoneassistedtreatment.org
Suboxone Assisted Treatment is a comprehensive site on buprenorphine containing clinic locators, state and federal regulations, patient success stories, and patient forums.

Psychotherapy
Psychotherapy, also known as individual counseling or cognitive behavioral therapy, seeks to address the psychological aspects of addiction. This is where the "heavy lifting" often takes place. Psychotherapy can help people unravel, understand, or process feelings that may have nothing to with their addictions directly, but often are invaluable.

Pyschotherapy is a must when it comes to addressing the inter-personal component of recovery.

Qigong
Qigong (pronounced "chee-gung;" also spelled chi kung) translates from the Chinese as "energy cultivation" or "working with the life energy." Qigong's main goal is to enhance a person's "qi" or "chi," or "life energy." It is a very old Chinese practice that uses breathing techniques, meditations, and postural exercises to achieve this "recharge."

Qigong may be used as a daily routine to increase well-being, as well as for disease prevention and stress reduction. It can be used to increase energy and reduce stress. In China, qigong is used commonly in conjunction with other medical therapies for many chronic conditions.

In the depleted state of an individual suffering with ongoing addiction, qigong can play a significant role in "recharging" the batteries.

Relationships (Social Medicine)
The importance of your interpersonal relationships cannot be overstated in the context of recovery. Having a spouse, friend, parent, counselor, etc. that you can contact when you are in a vulnerable state can be the difference between relapse and maintenance of your recovery. It's essential that you have people in your life that can understand, forgive, and support you during recovery.

See chapter 4 for more information about relationships.

Sleep
Restful sleep is an important part of overall health. If you do not achieve a deep sleep at night, you will be at increased risk for depression, anxiety, and other mental health disorders. Sleep provides an important time for the body to recharge, fuel the immune system, and process events of the day via the subconscious. A lack of sleep will prevent you from moving fully forward in recovery; your decision-making, impulse control, and overall thinking can be greatly disturbed.

Trauma Work

Trauma work can be defined as the introspection into one's past trauma. Trauma may be physical, mental, or both. Addiction may arise from a conscious or unconscious desire to escape past trauma. Trauma work helps to unfold any pathways that can be found that support long lasting healing and improvement in one's life. There are several different methods of trauma work, a few of which are described below.

Eye Movement Desensitization Reprocessing (EMDR)

Done with a therapist or practitioner that is EMDR certified, EMDR carries the proposition that while using an object for the eye to track, painful memories can be removed while talking to the therapist. Like hypnosis, EMDR can be a quick, in-office exercise that greatly enhances goals in therapy.

Neurolinguistic Programming (NLP)

NLP is the true marrying of hypnotherapy and psychotherapy. It uses different hypnotic and psychoanalytic approaches to confront conscious and subconscious beliefs about anything, including illness, self-esteem, world view.

NLP has helped to improve patients' relationships, communication, and work performance—all important pieces of a successful recovery strategy.

Dialectical Behavior Therapy (DBT)

DBT is usually designed specifically for people with bipolar personality disorder (BPD) and suicidal behavior. It is goal oriented, with emphasis on the recognition of one's behaviors and one's control of them. Studies have shown that people who practice DBT have fewer suicide attempts and enter the hospital less often. It is a modality often instituted with success when needed in substance abuse treatment.

Volunteering

Volunteering, or performing acts of service, has been recommended as a component of recovery for decades. Helping people who are facing different challenges allows you to draw focus outside of yourself.

Addiction often demands some strict introspection. It is easy to lose track of the community around you. Recovery has the reputation of being a very self-absorbed period of time. Often, it is this misconception that leads to isolation and despair.

The giving of your time may enable you to view your own addiction and co-occurring disorder(s) in a new light. Getting "out of your head" for a bit and experiencing gratitude for what you have can be vital tools in your daily recovery strategy.

In some, volunteering becomes a life's purpose, a vital element in their sobriety, a turn of a switch when it comes to supporting long lasting recovery.

Visit www.volunteermatch.org to locate volunteer opportunities in your community.

Yoga

The regular practice of yoga has been integral to countless recovery success stories. There are not many treatment strategies out there that capture the combination of mind, body, and spirit like yoga. When done over a period of time, the benefits can be seen on many levels. The opportunity to concentrate on your breathing, while stretching and strengthening your spine and muscles during a potential meditative state, is a fierce tool when it comes to treating addiction effectively.

There are many types of yoga. Often, people will find a practice that speaks to them after trying different classes.

Ananda Yoga

Ananda focuses on gentle postures that help to circulate the body's energy and prepare the body for meditation.

Ashtanga (or Astanga) Yoga

A more physically demanding style of yoga, Ashtanga involves a continuous series of postures that can produce increased internal heat, leading to detoxifying effects on the body and organs. This is not for beginners and is similar to an athletic practice.

Bikram Yoga

This style of yoga is practiced in a 95–105 degree temperature to enhance the detoxification effect and includes many components of overall fitness, including muscular strength, cardiovascular fitness, and weight loss.

Hatha Yoga

Probably the most popular form in the U.S., Hatha combines postures, breathing, and meditation into a complete system. Hatha is great for stress relief and good for beginners.

Kripalu Yoga

More a practice of introspection, the emphasis of Kripalu is on the holding of poses to explore and release blockages. Kripalu could be considered "meditation in motion."

Restorative Yoga

This style of yoga is very helpful with individuals who have had physical and mental trauma. Passively allowing muscles to relax, much of the time is spent lying on yoga blocks, blankets, and soft grounding.

Sivananda Yoga

This yoga combines postures and breathing with dietary restrictions, chanting, scriptural study, and meditation.

Svaroopa Yoga

This style of yoga is very user-friendly. Often, Svaroopa begins in a chair and the poses are comfortable and very accessible.

Viniyoga

Like restorative yoga, Viniyoga is very helpful for people who have suffered physical trauma and are recovering from surgical procedures. It is usually individualized to each person's needs.

" Breathe. Let go. And remind yourself that this very moment is the only one you know you have for sure."

–Oprah Winfrey

UNIT 4

LIFELONG RECOVERY BEYOND REHAB

We have examined the three core components that serve as the foundation for long-term recovery. We have explored the different healing modalities that can contribute to your overall success story. Now, how do you put this together? How do you manifest everything we have just discussed? How can you start your plan today? **If you are reading this, you already have.**

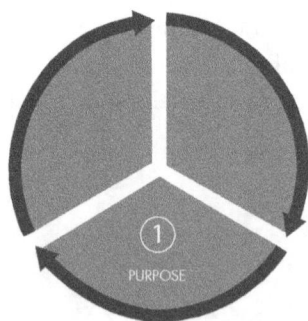

① PURPOSE

Your Purpose

Figuring out why a life without drug or alcohol abuse has greater reward than a life with it is essential. Be specific about your purpose—let it drive you forward. Take a moment to reflect on your purpose and again, write it down. Be specific. Compare it to your purpose statement from the beginning of the book.

_____

_____

_____

_____

_____

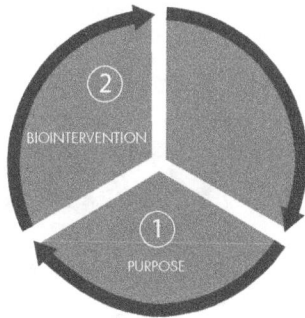

Biointervention

There are observed brain changes that occur after long-term, and in some cases even short-term, drug or alcohol abuse. Whether it is treating your addiction or treating a co-occurring condition, this must be addressed in one way or another. Addressing the biochemical factor is usually achieved through one, or some combination, of the following modalities:

-*Exercise*
-*Nutrition*
-*Nutraceuticals*
-*Medications*

Be specific. What has worked? What has not worked? What have you done? What have you not done? What are your concrete goals? In other words, be honest. There is no "happy" pill. We do not simply arrive one day at complete bliss. When life gets difficult, we fall back into old patterns and habits. You must forgive yourself for this before you can give an honest assessment of your needs.

Write down what biochemical intervention you are doing, what you plan to do, and even what has or has not worked for you in the past. Compare it to the one you did at the beginning of the book.

_____

_____

_____

_____

_____

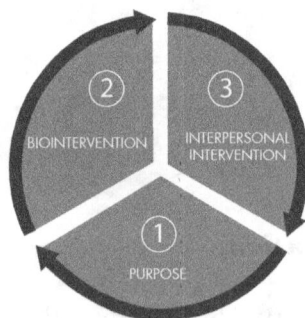

Interpersonal Intervention

You know why you want to stop abusing drugs or alcohol. You've leveled the playing field biochemically. This is where you must swallow the idea that recovery is very difficult to do alone.

You will have the best shot at long-term recovery from addiction if you are sincere and willing to trust even one person besides yourself. This is often reflected in:

-Individual counseling or therapy
-Group therapy
-Relationships

Write down which relationships support you in recovery and which do not. Who is your counselor or psychologist? What is his/her contact info? What is the schedule of the group therapies available in your community? Again, be specific. The more specific you are, the better the chances that you will commit to your plan. Compare it to the one you did at the beginning of the book.

_____

_____

_____

_____

_____

Once you've created your plan—one that integrates biochemical intervention, individual and group counseling, complementary modalities, treatment for any potential co-occurring disorders, and the drive to create continued recovery with a concrete purpose in mind—how do you move forward?

Moment by moment.

Day by day.

Lean on someone who can provide continual support, guidance, and encouragement, especially at the beginning.

Remind yourself why you are doing each part of your treatment plan. Staying focused on the motivation behind each modality will ensure that your treatment plan becomes ritual, and eventually part of your daily lifestyle. Be patient and forgive yourself if you slip up. Just keep going.

*" Wherever you go, go with all
your heart. "*

−Confucius

CHAPTER 9

STAYING ON TRACK

Most of us keep "to do" lists and schedules that remind us of important commitments. Likewise, you will probably find that such methods of organization are important to your recovery. After all, is this not the most important thing happening in your life right now?

The YOURecovery™ Journal is a guide to help you navigate your day. It will help you to continually prioritize your recovery and ideally create an ongoing self-audit of what works and what does not.

– Each day has its own page with a blank calendar at the top and an area on the bottom for directed journaling. The latter space is where you can continually formulate or reaffirm your daily biochemical intervention; your daily interpersonal intervention, giving priority to counseling; and your daily reminder as to why you are doing this in the first place.

– Each week has a page designated for reflection. This is where you can write down what you learned the previous week and/ or outline your objectives for the upcoming week.
– Each month has a page designated for goal-setting. This is

where you can write down what worked and what didn't work during the past month or where you can outline your goals for the next month.

Don't forget to document your "aha" moments and any nuggets of wisdom you gain from counseling.

While every journal looks different, they should all share some common elements:

– Accountability to the three essential components (Your Purpose, Biointervention, Interpersonal Intervention)

– Documentation of the complementary tools being used

– Record of what works and what does not

You may prefer to use your own composition book or keep track of your recovery electronically; it doesn't matter what technique you use—just use something!

Isn't it time to start prioritizing your success?

"It is difficult to make a man miserable while he feels worthy
of himself and claims kindred to the great God who made him."
Abraham Lincoln

SATURDAY **05**

JANUARY

6:00-7:00a	7:00-8:00a	8:00-9:00a	9:00-10:00a	10:00-11:00a	11:00-12:00p
12:00-1:00p	1:00-2:00p	2:00-3:00p	3:00-4:00p	4:00-5:00p	5:00-6:00p
6:00-7:00p	7:00-8:00p	8:00-9:00p	9:00-10:00p	10:00-11:00p	11:00-12:00a

TODAY, I FULFILL MY PURPOSE AND NURTURE MY SPIRIT...

DAILY PURPOSE GOALS

1. _____
2. _____
3. _____

TODAY, I CARE FOR MY BODY WITH FITNESS,
NUTRITION AND MEDICINAL NEEDS...

DAILY PHYSICAL GOALS

1. _____
2. _____
3. _____

DAILY INTERPERSONAL GOALS

1. _____
2. _____
3. _____

...TODAY, I REACH OUT, SUPPORT AND FEEL SUPPORTED BY OTHERS

"It is difficult to make a man miserable while he feels worthy of himself and claims kindred to the great God who made him."
Abraham Lincoln

SUNDAY	**30**	
MONDAY	**31**	
TUESDAY	**01**	
WEDNESDAY	**02**	
THURSDAY	**03**	
FRIDAY	**04**	
SATURDAY	**05**	

THIS WEEK, I FULFILL MY PURPOSE AND NURTURE MY SPIRIT...

WEEKLY PURPOSE GOALS

1.
2.
3.

THIS WEEK, I CARE FOR MY BODY WITH FITNESS, NUTRITION AND MEDICINAL NEEDS....

WEEKLY PHYSICAL GOALS

1.
2.
3.

WEEKLY INTERPERSONAL GOALS

1.
2.
3.

...THIS WEEK, I REACH OUT, SUPPORT AND FEEL SUPPORTED BY OTHERS

118

DECEMBER 2012

25	26	27	28	29	30	01

02	03	04	05	06	07	08

09	10	11	12	13	14	15

16	17	18	19	20	21	22

23	24	25	26	27	28	29

30	31

THIS MONTH, I FULFILL MY PURPOSE AND NURTURE MY SPIRIT...

MONTHLY PURPOSE GOALS
1. _____
2. _____
3. _____

THIS MONTH, I CARE FOR MY BODY WITH FITNESS, NUTRITION AND MEDICINAL NEEDS....

MONTHLY PHYSICAL GOALS
1. _____
2. _____
3. _____

MONTHLY INTERPERSONAL GOALS
1. _____
2. _____
3. _____

...THIS MONTH, I REACH OUT, SUPPORT AND FEEL SUPPORTED BY OTHERS

"You don't have to control your thoughts; you just have to stop letting them control you."

—Dan Millman

CHAPTER 10

THE PERFECT PLAN AND THE ART OF LIVING IT

Ok, you're ready to change.

You have given meaning and structure to the three essential components.

You are moving forward in your journal, documenting and learning every day.

You're doing great. But, you're not done.

Recovery is lifelong. It takes time, and often, trial and error. But, it doesn't have to be a battle forever. Successful recovery plans can lead to being recovered.

What's in a Word?
Recovery happens while people are living their lives—not while they are in detoxification or rehabilitation, not during an overdose, and not while intoxicated. But the word "recovery" has some strong connotations that may be frustrating to you. "Recovery" can imply that "I was really sick—so sick that for the rest of my life I need to recover."

However, it is important to understand the power of the phrase "lifelong recovery." The term suggests that your situation was severe; it also implies that you can rebuild, renew, and get better from a very serious disease state. Additionally, it serves as a daily reminder that this condition can still resurface—and it can be deadly.

If the word "recovery" prevents you from creating real life changes, then change the word. When "recovery" is used in this book, it is meant as a familiar phrase, not as a binding term. You may prefer to use "change," "redirection," "restoration," or "healing" to describe your situation. Never let the word be an obstacle to your success.

Moving Forward

Stories of recovery can range from those who have created long-term healing to those who are still seeking out that last piece of the puzzle. But many, if not all those who are working to overcome addiction, share the same desire: to reclaim their life.

If you would like to share your story with others, submit it on YOURecovery.com so we may confidentially include it in our newsletter. There's a good chance that an element of your story will speak to someone else and possibly plant a seed for a different long-term healing plan. Sharing supports our interconnectedness.

No matter where you are on the journey, stay focused on your goals and strategies. Let go of what does not work and incorporate into your plan what does. Keep your supporters close and your triggers as far away as possible.

People get better. You can get better. I see success stories every day. Let yours be one of them.

" Nothing is impossible, the word
itself says ' I'm possible!' "

-Audrey Hepburn

Afterword

I wrote this book because it poured out of me. It was written as a reaction to a very fragmented medical system that did not offer people the integration needed for successful outcomes. It was a reaction to a disease whose cure seemed elusive.

I needed to put it out there because of the success rates I was seeing in patients who employed the strategies outlined in this book. This book is for anyone—from the person just entering recovery to the person who has been sober for decades to the loved one of someone who is struggling with ongoing addiction or recovery.

Check out YOURecovery.com for resources, newsletters, and much more.

To YOU and YOUR RECOVERY!

Dr. Dubin

Appendix A

YOURecovery's ™ Top 10 List for Long-term Success

1. Don't Go It Alone

Ideally, you have friends, a spouse, a parent, or a child who love you unconditionally. They may be feeling angry, frustrated, and helpless as you struggle with addiction, but they still love you. Relationships with these people may no longer seem possible. At the same time, you may be surprised to discover that people you've disappointed are still eager to help you. Even if all you have is a sponsor, a counselor, or a health care provider—people need people. Be bold and allow yourself to trust someone close to you.

Having the support of someone else is crucial, especially during those difficult early days when recovery seems impossible. Be patient if your loved ones don't know how to help, and ask them to have patience with you. Nar-Anon (www.nar-anon. org) and Al-Anon (www.al-anon.org) are great resources for family members and friends of loved ones with addiction.

2. Nutrition

Understanding the impact of proper nutrition on your recovery from addiction is vital. Aside from decreased appetite, long-term addiction can lead to gastrointestinal disorders that include the eventual inability to digest and absorb foods properly. During recovery, your body will most likely crave foods that are high in nutrients so it can rebuild damaged tissues and organs and reestablish proper functioning of the nervous and gastrointestinal systems. Do not underestimate proper nutrition on a daily basis. Get help with this if you need it.

Additionally, food affects mood. Proper nutrition actually impacts cravings for drugs and alcohol. Long-term addiction creates deficiencies in various amino acids such as tyrosine, glutamine, and tryptophan as well as nutrients like B-complex vitamins and folic acid. As building blocks for the production of important neurotransmitters, decreased levels of amino acids can negatively affect mood and behavior. In turn, using drugs and alcohol appears more attractive. It's a vicious cycle.

Proper supplementation is often essential for improved mental clarity, emotional stability, well-being, and long-term recovery. Sugar and caffeine intake can add to the overall impact of these imbalances; their elimination or decreased use may be essential for your long-term recovery.

3. Sleep

Multiple studies show the importance of restful sleep in order to maintain good health. When it comes to addiction, most people do not achieve the deep sleep necessary for proper cognitive functioning. Of course, if you can't think properly, you won't be able to pay attention in counseling, get to your health care provider on time, or employ the valuable recovery strategies you have created and need. What's more, a lack of good sleep may increase the attractiveness of drugs or alcohol. Sleep allows for the proper hormonal stability and balancing that is integral to successful recovery. There is much debate on how much sleep we need, but the latest research points to this amount: whatever is enough for you.

4. Detoxification

Not everyone needs to be in detox to start down the path to recovery. Still, many people need to go through either a safe stay at a detoxification facility or an at-home detox during which time their offending addictive agent is removed. This creates the platform for what comes next. In fact, unless the addictive agent is removed, it is difficult to assess what may have led to addiction in the first place.

However, some treatments may be started before this. Making that phone call to your health care provider or telling your spouse about your problem use—even while intoxicated—may help you tomorrow.

5. Attention to Brain Changes

Don't ignore potential changes in brain chemistry with long-standing abuse of drugs or alcohol. These changes can affect your brain's limbic system—the system that tells you to eat, drink, go to the bathroom, and have sex. Unless this piece is evaluated and potentially treated (either nutritionally, pharmaceutically, or both), the next step in recovery can be plagued by restlessness and extreme craving.

125

Not everyone needs medicine; in fact, often medicine is utilized to provide short-term or long-term biochemical stabilization so people can engage in their own treatment. These medicines, nutraceuticals, herbs, vitamins, or amino acids are geared towards the addiction at hand or the co-occurring disorder that may be fueling your addiction. Typically, these pharmaceutical tools can be tapered off after you have created the psychological, social, and emotional tools needed to prevent relapse in the future.

6. Attention to Co-Occurring Disorders

Do you have chronic pain? Depression? Anxiety? Attention deficit disorder? Bipolar disorder? Post traumatic stress disorder? Prolonged grief response?

It's possible you are using drugs or alcohol to self-medicate. Unfortunately, the risks outweigh the benefits. Many options exist when it comes to treating these conditions—from medicines to supplements to exercise to acupuncture. No addiction treatment plan is complete without an honest assessment and treatment of co-existing psychiatric conditions.

7. Talk Therapy

A great psychologist, counselor, or therapist is often the cornerstone of any comprehensive recovery program. Keep in mind that you need to find someone who resonates with you. If you don't feel comfortable trusting your therapist with your deep secrets, you will have a very lonely road towards recovery. A good therapist has most likely heard stories similar to yours. Don't be afraid to be honest. If you are talking about hockey or scrapbooking at the end of your first session, don't go back. This should be a serious, difficult session. Your therapist is usually a key relationship to get you through recovery. Find someone who challenges you while working for you and with you.

8. Group Therapy

Shared experiences can help you fill your own recovery tool box. You may not agree with everything that people say during a group therapy session, but you will develop the ability to discern which information is useful. This is an imperative skill to have in recovery. Knowing that you are not alone can help lay the foundation for real recovery. Don't be afraid to check out your local Alcoholics Anonymous or Narcotics Anonymous meeting; you may be surprised by what you gain from shared group meetings.

9. Exercise

Exercise, even in its mildest and shortest forms, is one of nature's most powerful tools to combat depression, anxiety, and addiction. The dopamine surge you get while exercising is similar to the surge felt under the influence of certain drugs. Don't use exercise just to replace your typical buzz with a healthier one, but remember that it may be part of your restorative process. Exercise can prepare the way for neurobiological repair that is needed for long-term recovery.

10. Know When to Ask for Help

Create a team of supporters that allows you to be honest regarding what you need. Often, an addiction medicine specialist or family primary care provider can help you determine your addiction severity based on real evidence-based criteria at any given time. Although you may be doing a wonderful job unlocking your personal recovery tool kit, actually using the tools can be challenging.

Appendix B

The Drug Abuse Screening Test (DAST)[1]

Directions: The following questions concern information about your involvement with drugs. Drug abuse refers to (1) the use of prescribed or "over-the-counter" drugs in excess of the directions, and (2) any non-medical use of drugs. Consider the past year (12 months) and carefully read each statement. Then decide whether your answer is YES or NO and write your answer in the space following the question. Please be sure to answer every question.

YES or NO

1. Have you used drugs other than those required for medical reasons? _____
2. Have you abused prescription drugs? _____
3. Do you abuse more than one drug at a time? _____
4. Can you get through the week without using drugs (other than those required for medical reasons)? _____
5. Are you always able to stop using drugs when you want to? _____
6. Do you abuse drugs on a continuous basis? _____
7. Do you try to limit your drug use to certain situations? _____
8. Have you had "blackouts" or "flashbacks" as a result of drug use? _____
9. Do you ever feel bad about your drug abuse? _____
10. Does your spouse (or parents) ever complain about your involvement with drugs? _____
11. Do your friends or relatives know or suspect you abuse drugs? _____
12. Has drug abuse ever created problems between you and your spouse? _____
13. Has any family member ever sought help for problems related to your drug use? _____
14. Have you ever lost friends because of your use of drugs? _____

---

1. Reprinted with permission from Elsevier Science. Skinner, Addictive Behaviors, 1982.

15. Have you ever neglected your family or missed work because of your use of drugs? _____
16. Have you ever been in trouble at work because of drug abuse? _____
17. Have you ever lost a job because of drug abuse? _____
18. Have you gotten into fights when under the influence of drugs? _____
19. Have you ever been arrested because of unusual behavior while under the influence of drugs? _____
20. Have you ever been arrested for driving while under the influence of drugs? _____
21. Have you engaged in illegal activities in order to obtain drug? _____
22. Have you ever been arrested for possession of illegal drugs? _____
23. Have you ever experienced withdrawal symptoms as a result of heavy drug intake? _____
24. Have you had medical problems as a result of your drug use (e.g., memory loss, hepatitis, convulsions, bleeding, etc.)? _____
25. Have you ever gone to anyone for help for a drug problem? _____
26. Have you ever been in a hospital for medical problems related to your drug use? _____
27. Have you ever been involved in a treatment program specifically related to drug use? _____
28. Have you been treated as an outpatient for problems related to drug abuse? _____

Scoring and interpretation:

A score of "1" is given for each YES response, except for items 4, 5, and 7, for which a NO response is given a score of "1."

6 through 11: very probable substance use disorder(s)

Over 12 : definitely a substance abuse problem

The Alcohol Use Disorders Identification Test (AUDIT)

1. How often do you have a drink containing alcohol?
[ ] Never (0) [Skip to Questions 9–10]
[ ] Monthly or less (1)
[ ] 2 to 4 times a month (2)
[ ] 2 to 3 times a week (3)
[ ] 4 or more times a week (4)

2. How many drinks containing alcohol do you have on a typical day when you are drinking?
[ ] 1 or 2 (0)
[ ] 3 or 4 (1)
[ ] 5 or 6 (2)
[ ] 7, 8, or 9 (3)
[ ] 10 or more (4)

3. How often do you have six or more drinks on one occasion?
[ ] Never (0)
[ ] Less than monthly (1)
[ ] Monthly (2)
[ ] Weekly (3)
[ ] Daily or almost daily (4)
[Skip to Questions 9 and 10 if Total Score for Questions 2 and 3 = 0]

4. How often during the last year have you found that you were unable to stop drinking once you had started?
[ ] Never (0)
[ ] Less than monthly (1)
[ ] Monthly (2)
[ ] Weekly (3)
[ ] Daily or almost daily (4)

5. How often during the last year have you failed to do what was normally expected of you because of drinking?
[ ] Never (0)
[ ] Less than monthly (1)
[ ] Monthly (2)
[ ] Weekly (3)
[ ] Daily or almost daily (4)

6. How often during the last year have you needed a first drink in the morning to get yourself going after a heavy drinking session?
[ ] Never (0)
[ ] Less than monthly (1)
[ ] Monthly (2)
[ ] Weekly (3)
[ ] Daily or almost daily (4)

7. How often during the last year have you had a feeling of guilt or remorse after drinking?
[ ] Never (0)
[ ] Less than monthly (1)
[ ] Monthly (2)
[ ] Weekly (3)
[ ] Daily or almost daily (4)

8. How often during the last year have you been unable to remember what happened the night before because you had been drinking?
[ ] Never (0)
[ ] Less than monthly (1)
[ ] Monthly (2)
[ ] Weekly (3)
[ ] Daily or almost daily (4)

9. Have you or someone else been injured as the result of your drinking?
[ ] No (0)
[ ] Yes, but not in the last year (1)
[ ] Yes, during the last year (2)

10. Has a relative, friend, or a doctor or other health worker been concerned about your drinking or suggested you cut down?
[ ] No (0)
[ ] Yes, but not in the last year (1)
[ ] Yes, in the last year (2)

Record the total of the specific items. _____

131

Scoring and Interpretation of the AUDIT

The minimum score (for nondrinkers) is 0 and the maximum possible score is 40.

A score of 8 is indicative of hazardous and harmful alcohol use, and possibly of alcohol dependence. Scores of 8–15 indicate a medium level and scores of 16 and above a high level of alcohol problems.

Again, keep in mind that this is a starting point for assessing your situation; a lower score may still be cause for concern.

Appendix C

DSM-V Criteria for Substance Use Disorders

Substance use disorders span a wide variety of problems arising from substance use, and cover 11 different criteria:

1. Taking the substance in larger amounts or for longer than the you meant to

2. Wanting to cut down or stop using the substance but not managing to

3. Spending a lot of time getting, using, or recovering from use of the substance

4. Cravings and urges to use the substance

5. Not managing to do what you should at work, home or school, because of substance use

6. Continuing to use, even when it causes problems in relationships

7. Giving up important social, occupational or recreational activities because of substance use

8. Using substances again and again, even when it puts the you in danger

9. Continuing to use, even when the you know you have a physical or psychological problem that could have been caused or made worse by the substance

10. Needing more of the substance to get the effect you want (tolerance)

11. Development of withdrawal symptoms, which can be relieved by taking more of the substance.

Two or three symptoms indicate a mild substance use disorder, four or five symptoms indicate a moderate substance use disorder, and six or more symptoms indicate a severe substance use disorder. Clinicians can also add "in early remission," "in sustained remission," "on maintenance therapy," and "in a controlled environment."

References

Akhondzadeh S. Kashani L, et al. "Passionflower in the treatment of opiates withdrawal: a double-blind randomized controlled trial." Journal of Clinical Pharmacy & Therapeutics. 26(5): 369-73, 2001.

Altern Ther Health Med 1997 Jul; 3(4): 57-66. Comparing Hatha yoga with dynamic group psychotherapy for enhancing methadone maintenance treatment: a randomized clinical trial.

American Psychiatric Association. Diagnostic and statistical manual of mental disorders. 4th ed. Washington, DC: APA, 2000.

Avants SK. Margolin A. Holford TR. Kosten TR. "A randomized controlled trial of auricular acupuncture for cocaine dependence." Archives of Internal Medicine. 160(15): 2305-12, 2000.

Baltimore, MD. Substance abuse: clinical problems and perspectives. William & Wilkins, 1981:317–38.

Beasley J.D. Diagnosing and Managing Chemical Dependency. Amityville, New York (2002).

Beasley, J.D. et al. Follow-up of a cohort of alcoholic patients through 12 months of comprehensive biobehavioral treatment. J Subst Abuse Treat 8, 133-42 (1991).

Bickel WK, Amass L. Buprenorphine treatment of opioid dependence: a review. Exp Clin Psychopharmacol 1995;3:477–89.

Blum K, Ross J, Reuben C, Gastelu D, Miller DK. "Nutritional Gene Therapy: Natural Healing in Recovery. Counselor Magazine, January/February, 2001

Blum, K. et al. Enkephalinase inhibition and precursor amino acid loading improves inpatient treatment of alcohol and polydrug abusers: double-blind placebo-controlled study of the nutritional adjunct SAAVE. Alcohol 5, 481-93 (1988).

Blum, K. et al. Reward deficiency syndrome: a biogenetic model for the diagnosis and treatment of impulsive, addictive, and compulsive behaviors. J Psychoactive Drugs 32 Suppl, i-iv, 1-112 (2000).

Bowden, S., Bardenhagen, F., Ambrose, M., and Whelan, G. Alcohol, thiamin deficiency, and neuropsychological disorders. Alcohol Suppl 2, 267-72 (1994).

Brown, R.J., Blum, K., and Trachtenberg, M.C. Neurodynamics of relapse prevention: a neuronutrient approach to outpatient DUI offenders. J Psychoactive Drugs 22, 173-87 (1990).

Cami, J. and Farre, M. Drug addiction. N Engl J Med 349, 975-86 (2003).

Carney, M.W. et al. Red cell folate concentrations in psychiatric patients. J Affect Disord 19, 207-13 (1990).

Elnimr, T., Hashem, A., and Assar, R. Heroin dependence effects on some major and trace elements. Biol Trace Elem Res 54, 153-62 (1996).

Free, V. and Sanders, P. The use of ascorbic acid and mineral supplements in the detoxifi-cation of narcotic addicts. J Psychedelic Drugs 11, 217-22 (1979).

Fudala PJ, Bridge TP, Herbert S, et al. Office-based treatment of opiate addiction with a sublingual-tablet formulation of buprenorphine and naloxone. N Engl J Med 2003; 349:949–58.

Girault, J.A. and Greengard, P. The neurobiology of dopamine signaling. Arch Neurol 61, 641-4 (2004).

Griffith, H.W. Complete Guide to Vitamins Minerals and Supplements. Fisher, Tucson, Arizona (1988).

Guenther, R.M. The role of nutritional therapy in alcoholism treatment. Int Journal of Biosocial Research 4, 5-18 (1983).

Johnson RE, Chutuape MA, Strain EC, Walsh SL, Stitzer ML, Bigelow GE. A comparison of levomethadyl acetate, buprenorphine and methadone for opioid dependence. N Engl J Med 2000; 343:1290–7.

Johnston LD, O'Malley PM, Bachman JG, Schulenberg JE. Monitoring the Future: national results on adolescent drug use: overview of key findings, 2003 [NIH pub. no. 04-5506]. Bethesda, MD: National Institute on Drug Abuse, 2004.

Kahan M. Treatment with vitamins, minerals and diet. Managing alcohol, tobacco and other drug problems: A pocket guide for physicians and nurses. 2002. Toronto, Canada, Centre for Addiction and Mental Health. Kahan, M. and Wilson, L. 82.

Kleber HD. Pharmacologic treatments for heroin and cocaine dependence. Am J Addict 2003:12(suppl): S1–4.

Kosten, T.R. Neurobiology of abused drugs. Opioids and stimulants. J Nerv Ment Dis 178, 217-27 (1990).

Krantz MJ, Mehler PS. Treating opioid dependence. Growing implications for primary care. Arch Intern Med 2004; 164:277

Li M, Chen K, Mo Z. "Use of qigong therapy in the detoxification of heroin addicts." Alternative Therapies in Health and Medicine. 8(1): 50-59, 2002.

Logan AC. Omega-3 fatty acids and major depression: a primer for the mental health professional. Lipids Health Dis 3, (2004).

Lohman R. "Yoga techniques applicable within drug and alcohol rehabilitation programmes." Therapeutic Communities. 20(1): 61-71, 1999.

Majumdar, S.K., Shaw, G.K., and Thomson, A.D. Vitamin utilization status in chronic alcoholics. Int J Vitam Nutr Res 51, 54-8 (1981).

Manari, A.P., Preedy, V.R., and Peters, T.J. Nutritional intake of hazardous drinkers and dependent alcoholics in the UK. Addict Biol 8, 201-10 (2003).

Mason, A.P. and McBay, A.J. Cannabis: pharmacology and interpretation of effects. J Forensic Sci 30, 615-31 (1985).

Mathews-Larson, J. and Parker, P.A. Alcoholism treatment with a biochemical restoration as a major component. Int J Biosoc Res 9, 92-106 (1987).

McCance-Katz EF, Kosten TR. Psychopharmacological treatments. In: Miller S, Frances R, eds. Clinical textbook of addictive disorders. 2nd ed. New York: Guilford, 1998: 596-624.

McCance-Katz EF, Kosten TR. Psychopharmacological treatments. In: Miller S, Frances R, eds. Clinical textbook of addictive disorders. 3rd ed. New York: Guilford (in press).

Mee-Lee D, ed. ASAM patient placement criteria for the treatment of substance-related disorders. 2nd ed. rev. Chevy Chase, MD: American Society of Addiction Medicine, 2001.

Miller, C.S. Toxicant-induced loss of tolerance. Addiction 96, 115-37 (2001).

Mohs, M.E., Watson, R.R., and Leonard-Green, T. Nutritional effects of marijuana, heroin, cocaine, and nicotine. J Am Diet Assoc 90, 1261-7 (1990).

Moos, R.H., King, M.J., Burnett, E.B., and Andrassy, J.M. Community residential program policies, services, and treatment orientations influence patients' participation in treatment. J Subst Abuse 9, 171-87 (1997).

Morabia, A. et al. Diet and opiate addiction: a quantitative assessment of the diet of non-institutionalized opiate addicts. Br J Addict 84, 173-80 (1989).

Nazrul Islam, S.K., Jahangir Hossain, K., and Ahsan, M. Serum vitamin E, C and A status of the drug addicts undergoing detoxification: influence of drug habit, sexual practice and lifestyle factors. Eur J Clin Nutr 55, 1022-7 (2001).

Oak, J.N., Oldenhof, J., and Van Tol, H.H. The dopamine D(4) receptor: one decade of research. Eur J Pharmacol 405, 303 27 (2000).

Odeleye O.E. and Watson R.R. Role of nutrition in alcoholism. J Appl Nutr 44, 50-62 (1992).

Peet, M. and Stokes, C. Omega-3 fatty acids in the treatment of psychiatric disorders. Drugs 65, 1051-9 (2005).

Position of the American Dietetic Association. Nutrition intervention in treatment and recovery from chemical dependency. J Am Diet Assoc 90, 1274-7 (1990).

Johnston LD, O'Malley PM, Bachman JG, Schulenberg JE. Monitoring the Future: national results on adolescent drug use: overview of key findings, 2003 [NIH pub. no. 04-5506]. Bethesda, MD: National Institute on Drug Abuse, 2004.

Kahan M. Treatment with vitamins, minerals and diet. Managing alcohol, tobacco and other drug problems: A pocket guide for physicians and nurses. 2002. Toronto, Canada, Centre for Addiction and Mental Health. Kahan, M. and Wilson, L. 82.

Kleber HD. Pharmacologic treatments for heroin and cocaine dependence. Am J Addict 2003:12(suppl): S1–4.

Kosten, T.R. Neurobiology of abused drugs. Opioids and stimulants. J Nerv Ment Dis 178, 217-27 (1990).

Krantz MJ, Mehler PS. Treating opioid dependence. Growing implications for primary care. Arch Intern Med 2004; 164:277

Li M, Chen K, Mo Z. "Use of qigong therapy in the detoxification of heroin addicts." Alternative Therapies in Health and Medicine. 8(1): 50-59, 2002.

Logan AC. Omega-3 fatty acids and major depression: a primer for the mental health professional. Lipids Health Dis 3, (2004).

Lohman R. "Yoga techniques applicable within drug and alcohol rehabilitation programmes." Therapeutic Communities. 20(1): 61-71, 1999.

Majumdar, S.K., Shaw, G.K., and Thomson, A.D. Vitamin utilization status in chronic alcoholics. Int J Vitam Nutr Res 51, 54-8 (1981).

Manari, A.P., Preedy, V.R., and Peters, T.J. Nutritional intake of hazardous drinkers and dependent alcoholics in the UK. Addict Biol 8, 201-10 (2003).

Mason, A.P. and McBay, A.J. Cannabis: pharmacology and interpretation of effects. J Forensic Sci 30, 615-31 (1985).

Mathews-Larson, J. and Parker, P.A. Alcoholism treatment with a biochemical restoration as a major component. Int J Biosoc Res 9, 92-106 (1987).

McCance-Katz EF, Kosten TR. Psychopharmacological treatments. In: Miller S, Frances R, eds. Clinical textbook of addictive disorders. 2nd ed. New York: Guilford, 1998: 596–624.

McCance-Katz EF, Kosten TR. Psychopharmacological treatments. In: Miller S, Frances R, eds. Clinical textbook of addictive disorders. 3rd ed. New York: Guilford (in press).

Mee-Lee D, ed. ASAM patient placement criteria for the treatment of substance-related disorders. 2nd ed. rev. Chevy Chase, MD: American Society of Addiction Medicine, 2001.

Miller, C.S. Toxicant-induced loss of tolerance. Addiction 96, 115-37 (2001).

Mohs, M.E., Watson, R.R., and Leonard-Green, T. Nutritional effects of marijuana, heroin, cocaine, and nicotine. J Am Diet Assoc 90, 1261-7 (1990).

Moos, R.H., King, M.J., Burnett, E.B., and Andrassy, J.M. Community residential program policies, services, and treatment orientations influence patients' participation in treatment. J Subst Abuse 9, 171-87 (1997).

Morabia, A. et al. Diet and opiate addiction: a quantitative assessment of the diet of non-institutionalized opiate addicts. Br J Addict 84, 173-80 (1989).

Nazrul Islam, S.K., Jahangir Hossain, K., and Ahsan, M. Serum vitamin E, C and A status of the drug addicts undergoing detoxification: influence of drug habit, sexual practice and lifestyle factors. Eur J Clin Nutr 55, 1022-7 (2001).

Oak, J.N., Oldenhof, J., and Van Tol, H.H. The dopamine D(4) receptor: one decade of research. Eur J Pharmacol 405, 303-27 (2000).

Odeleye O.E. and Watson R.R. Role of nutrition in alcoholism. J Appl Nutr 44, 50-62 (1992).

Peet, M. and Stokes, C. Omega-3 fatty acids in the treatment of psychiatric disorders. Drugs 65, 1051-9 (2005).

Position of the American Dietetic Association. Nutrition intervention in treatment and recovery from chemical dependency. J Am Diet Assoc 90, 1274-7 (1990).

Tomkins, D.M. and Sellers, E.M. Addiction and the brain: the role of neurotransmitters in the cause and treatment of drug dependence. CMAJ 164, 817-21 (2001).

Trachtenberg, M.C. and Blum, K. Improvement of cocaine-induced neuromodulator deficits by the neuronutrient Tropamine. J Psychoactive Drugs 20, 315-31 (1988).

Van den Berg, H., van der Gaag, M., and Hendriks, H. Influence of lifestyle on vitamin bioavailability. Int J Vitam Nutr Res 72, 53-9 (2002).

Williams, R. Alcoholism The Nutritional Approach. University of Texas Press, Austin, TX (1959).

Williams, R.J. Physicians' Handbook of Nutritional Science. Charles C. Thomas, Illinois (1978).

Young, S.N. and Leyton, M. The role of serotonin in human mood and social interaction. Insight from altered tryptophan levels. Pharmacol Biochem Behav 71, 857-65 (2002).

Young, S.N. and Sourkes, T.L. Antidepressant action of tryptophan. Lancet 2, 897-8 (1974).

Index

145

VISIT
WWW.YOURECOVERY.COM
FOR MORE RESOURCES!

YOURecovery.com has been created to assist people in building their successful recovery story.

YOURecovery.com has been put together as a response to a very fragmented medical system, a condition that seems to have an elusive cure, and a disease that demands an individualized and integrated approach. YOURecovery.com honors the observation that most people's successful long-term recovery strategies are unique and may change throughout their lives.

The mission includes education on topics of addiction and recovery, online access to essential tools for recovery, as well as an unwavering commitment to continual improvement; in other words, the staff at YOURecovery.com is in constant forward progress mode. We welcome and encourage new information and new advances in the field of addiction medicine.

May this website be a resource for you and your family. To you and YOURecovery™!

www.ingramcontent.com/pod-product-compliance
Lightning Source LLC
LaVergne TN
LVHW021504080426
835509LV00018B/2389